Lifescapes

Lifescapes

Garden designs for your lifestyle

Sven Wombwell

For Camilla

First published in Great Britain by Simon & Schuster UK Ltd, 2004
A Viacom Company

Simon & Schuster UK Ltd
Africa House
64–78 Kingsway
London
WC2B 6AH

2 4 6 8 10 9 7 5 3 1

Designed for Simon & Schuster by:
Eye For Design
The Barn, Tye Green
Elsenham, Nr Bishop's Stortford
Hertfordshire CM22 6DY

Managing Editor: Nicki Lampon
Copy Editor: Anna Hitchen

A CIP catalogue record of this book is available from the British Library

ISBN 07432 6347 2

Printed and bound in China
by RR Donnelley

Contents

Anticipating the life we'll live tomorrow

Life has never stood still, but now the pace of change is accelerating dramatically. Our expectations of life at work and at home have changed beyond recognition. The influences on the clothes we wear, the food we eat and the environment we live in are many, complex and global. As people, our choices and behaviour can no longer be predicted by tidy classifications of age, class or geography. We don't follow every fad and fashion – we pick and choose and mould to suit our needs.

One thing is certain – the way we live is changing and we are becoming far more demanding in what we want and need as individuals, even if we don't always know exactly what we want. This book looks at today's trends and their implications, but it is not trying to produce a set of templates for 'the garden of tomorrow' – each garden and each gardener is, and always will be, unique. The aim is to share some insights and, hopefully, provide some inspiration for creating gardens that people can live with, live in and love well into the future.

Space and lifestyle

Space is now at a premium and, with more and more people being squeezed into towns and cities, we are realising that every square inch we have needs to be used to its full potential. Gardens are therefore now becoming an even more important part of life – as shelter, refuge, hobby or simply another 'room' of the house. All our choices speak volumes about who we are and what we want from the space. Our homes are increasingly becoming spaces designed to suit and support a way of life; a home is now more than just a roof over our heads. Stylish home accessories are much cheaper these days and far more readily available, allowing us to create home and garden 'makeovers' without breaking the bank. Large stores such as Ikea and Habitat now offer people a 'lifestyle' and not just simple furniture – it's that 'lifestyle' that people are buying into and this is down to a number of different factors. The availability of cheaper 'designer' products has exploded over the last half century. Shops such as Habitat, founded by the furniture designer Terence Conran, offer people a chance to have stylish and contemporary items previously out of reach. This applies not only to interiors, but also to fashion, food, and even cars – all the luxury elements in life. All the lifestyle shows on TV are inspiring more and more people to have a go at home improvement themselves and people have far more knowledge about the design process and how to go about it. This is especially obvious in the UK where sales of DIY products have risen dramatically over recent years.

Today more than ever, gardens are designed to suit the lifestyles that people lead. Even if you want a traditional garden full of herbaceous borders or tender plants, what is the point if you can't look after it? Unless you can afford a gardener, of course! The term 'low maintenance' is something I hear used more and more frequently by the people I design for. There is a garden to suit everyone and, if carefully designed, it will fit in with your busy schedule. Also a garden is a space upon which you can stamp your own personality. Don't let the space scare you and become overwhelming – take it slowly, perhaps even deal with one section at a time. Of course, every person is different and what you want from the space will be entirely individual, but there are rules that are proven to work. On the other hand, rules are there to be broken. A garden is something that can take time to develop and in my mind this is often a good thing. They say good things come to those who wait and in gardening this is especially true.

Personalising a garden design

My garden is the perfect example of a space designed to suit a 'lifestyle'. Because of my job I am away from home a lot of the time, and the last thing I want to do is spend all my spare time working in my own garden when I spend my life doing other people's! It took me two weeks to build my garden from scratch and I must admit it took me ages to come up with a final design. Because I had so many ideas in my head from other designs I had done, I kept changing my mind about what it should look like. In the end, I went for a garden that is a combination of a few of the ten gardens in this book. Firstly, it had to be an 'easy' garden, which would need little maintenance, so I dispensed with a lawn and decided on red wood decking throughout. It has elements of the 'exotic garden' in terms of some of the plants. But many exotics are hard work to look after so I chose hardy and semi-hardy exotics that I know will survive in my sheltered garden such as tree ferns, date palms and heavenly bamboo. It has a 'designer garden' feel with modern-looking benches with lights in them – this was purely down to personal taste and I guess it reflects my own style of garden design. That is part of the beauty of designing an outdoor space: you are far less restricted than you are inside the home, and to create your ideal space, you can mix and match different styles to suit different lifestyle needs.

Choosing a garden to suit you

People can't be put into strict categories, but in this book we have identified seven cultural trends that will increasingly influence the way people think. We will guide you through the design process in terms of 'what type of person you are', and this should help you decide on 'what type of garden will suit you'.

lifestyle trends

Anticipating the life we'll live tomorrow

I've been working with specialist forecasters and Marshalls plc and we have identified seven major trends in consumer attitudes and behaviour. These provide the key to predicting people's needs in the future – emotional as well as rational. They are based on a rigorous analysis of data on life and work from across the industrialised world and the views of a wide range of experts on buying patterns and lifestyle changes.

I'm not talking here about the far-off future gazing of an Arthur C Clarke nor the short-term micro trends which look at fads and fashions that come and go within a year or two. Those types of trends, however enjoyable or well-publicised, are of relatively limited use in understanding how gardens could develop in the future.

The trends included here reflect the beginnings of major changes in society and the way we behave, which are already being felt today, and will continue to change over the next 5-10 years if not longer.

Although I don't agree with the idea of pigeon holing people into groups as all

people are totally individual, we are inevitably influenced by trends and you will probably find elements within our seven trends that apply to you. But one or two will invariably dominate in determining what you want from your living environment and, most particularly, what role the garden plays in your life: what you want to be able to use it for and what satisfaction you want it to bring.

Just to reiterate my point not everyone will be affected by every trend, but nor are they mutually exclusive. They don't neatly divide up the population into seven 'types' – life isn't so simple or so compartmentalised.

Gardens are now more than ever a statement about lifestyle and if you can understand what your 'wants' are in terms of the way you live, then we can help you create a garden that will fit in with the lifestyle you lead.

The seven trends

- Quick living
- Life and more
- Air of tranquility
- New frontiers
- Together society
- Breathe easy
- Womanspace

trend 1 quick living

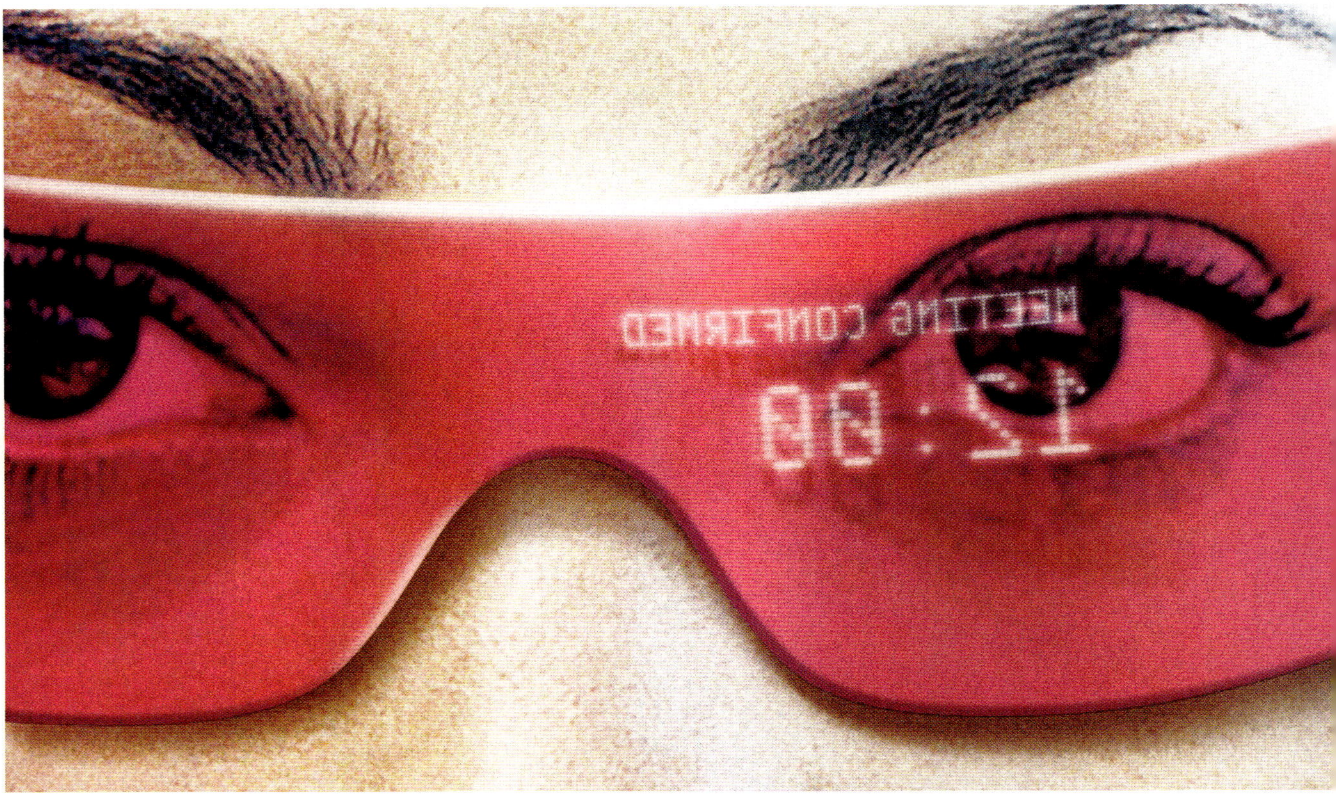

More and more we seem to be developing into a society where there isn't time for hanging about. The 'quick living' trend is all about those people who are always on the move, where life is all about pace, and keeping up to the minute. Mobile phones, email, video messaging, etc. mean we are always contactable wherever we are, because being out of touch is being out of the game and every second counts.

It can feel like everything in life is rush, rush, rush, and multi-tasking is the only way you can get things done, therefore, any technological advances that help things along and make life easier are essential, especially if they take care of things around the home so you don't have to.

Because we have become an increasingly no-time-to-wait culture, instant gratification is a must. Our lives are becoming increasingly streamlined for example, we are choosing to meet our partners through the Internet and Speed Dating – and so intelligent environments within the home have been developed to make not only our lives easier but to run itself too.

Too much automation sounds like a nightmare to me, but if you live this kind of lifestyle then just think how much time you could save – everything in life is so rushed, anything that makes things a little easier will be a great asset.

trend 2 air of tranquility

Are you the type of person who questions the Western 'have it all' consumer lifestyle and is concerned about the effects it has on your health and on the world's dwindling natural resources? You might be looking for an antidote to all things artificial and seeking calm and balance in a more natural way of life.

ɔu might not be the kind of person ıat will actively protest and join emonstrations to save the world, but ɔu will 'do your bit' in everyday life. nd when it comes to GM food and ther new fangled food technologies ɔu see it as 'messing with nature', so ɔu are more likely to head straight to ıe organic food counters in the shops. here are more and more people with ıis attitude which is reflected in the ıct that organic food counters in ıpermarkets are no longer just a tiny ɛction in the corner, but whole isles edicated to the organic produce. ɔu will also be likely to buy simple, ıthentic ingredients and styles from ıltures more in tune with nature and atural balance; this applies to both ɔoking and the interior of your home.

ɔu are the type of person that wants ɔ show respect to the environment, ıd avoid anything artificial, eat local roduce where possible and try to ıake time for contemplation.

You'll be searching for a more spiritual way of living, turning to ancient cultures for guidance, and also adopting a simpler way of life. More and more, you'll be benefiting from alternative therapies and natural remedies, even down to the way you exercise, which is now a way of strengthening the mind as well as the body with things like Pilates, yoga, and Tai-chi.
This all sounds very idealistic and in these modern times it is almost impossible to completely live life with this philosophy, not through want of trying, but quitting the rat race and dumping the microwave is not a realistic option for most. But through creating more space in your life for contemplation and balance, you will live a more natural way of life creating an air of tranquillity.

trend 3 together society

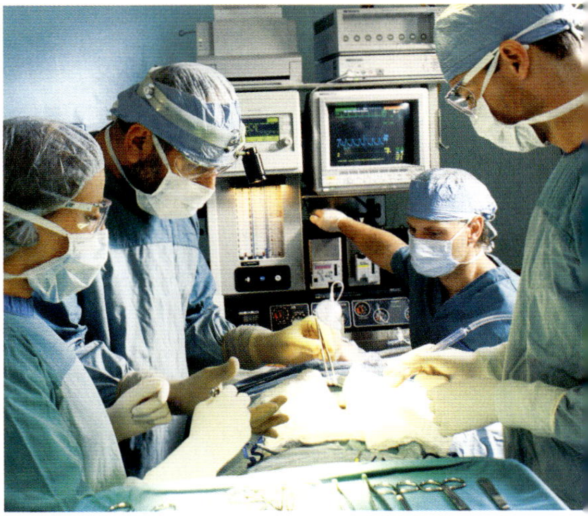

The idea of a traditional community is breaking down and being replaced by new alternatives, the old school community spirit is almost a thing of the past. Through breakthroughs in the way we communicate, social groups are more streamlined and based on shared interests and attitudes rather than geography. It is a sad fact that you may communicate with some bloke called Bob who lives on the other side of the world more than you do your neighbour – I know I'm guilty of that! I've got friends from all over the place, such as Australia, Sweden, and America, that I have not seen for years but I still know all that is going on with them, as if I saw them every weekend down the pub.

This has meant that cultural influences are spreading rapidly from country to country making people determined to protect the best of local against the diluting of culture through globalisation.

More people are choosing to marry later, if at all, and children are living with parents until much later in life well into their 20s. Working in an office is no longer a necessity and working from home and communicating through email, video phone and chat lines are becoming the norm. Because of this, people are creating their own ways of getting together with their chosen 'community', be it electronically or face to face, in a tailored environment to suit their work and home life.
It is really quite ironic that in the 'together' society you can 'get together' without actually being together at all.

trend 4 womanspace

What women want and their needs have changed dramatically over the years. Nowadays, juggling a career, home life, motherhood, friends, etc., is no small task (I would imagine), but with all these things to juggle, personal fulfilment may be hard to maintain.

This type of woman is right at home with what was once considered a male world with things like DIY, cars and sport without losing the feminine touch. Family is central to life and she has always kept contact with friends even back from the days at school and university – something which I've never managed to do!

Within the 'womanspace trend', everything is organised so that all your roles can be squeezed into what little time each day holds, and what you buy is designed to make the juggling act that little bit easier. But you try to make sure that there is also time for relaxation and plenty of personal indulgence.

Even in this 'Golden Age' life is a challenge on many different levels so anything that makes things easier and more organised so that you have more time for 'you', then bring it on.

trend 5 life and more

Medical advances have meant that people live longer and are healthier; this has given older people the freedom to lead far more active and adventurous lives. Now when people retire it in no way means the end, it is the beginning of a new life with more and more people opting to seek adventure and new experiences. There has been a massive increase in spending by the over 55s in the travel industry and as a result these companies are targeting this as a boom industry.

Of course health does deteriorate, bones ache, taste and smell become less acute, but now this group are being targeted by retailers with products developed for their needs, from TVs to DIY and gardening tools (oh, the garden claw). Now companies are using these people's experiences of youth such as music and fashion as a powerful tool to make them live again.

These people will embrace getting a little older and live life to the full, with more time spent on travel. They are also greeting new technology with open arms – long gone are the days of the techno-phobic and this also has given them more freedom and new experiences.

trend 6 new frontiers

These kind of people are always on the hunt for new extreme experiences, much of what used to be the exclusive is now available to the majority, long-haul holidays, sky diving, white water rafting, husky sledging in Lapland, etc., almost to the extent where they are not considered extreme any more. So bring on the search for more extreme experiences to excite people's ever-growing thirst for the unusual, a trip to the North Pole or flying a Mig fighter jet - new ways in which to get a rush and challenge the mind.

As well as looking for new adventures, these people love to share their experiences with their friends and through bringing fantastic trophies and the unusual into their own home can relive these experiences. They're looking for the new exotic, whether it's dancing with Masi warriors or taking a long weekend to the Antarctic. Technology that makes life easier is not always enough, it has to make life more exiting by bringing virtual experience into the home.

This hunt for the unusual does not just apply to holidays and experiences, but to all elements of life from perfumes to food with companies always on the hunt for unfamiliar scents or flavours or a rare ingredient with amazing stories of its origin. There are even plant companies specialising in the unusual and I just bought a really rare palm that is almost extinct in the wild.

trend 7 breathe easy

People are more than ever feeling pressure to 'have it all' and this means they need to cram as much as possible into every moment of life. This fast pace of living comes at a price and eventually you'll end up burnt out, so rather than slowing down people are looking for quick fix solutions – instant solutions for health and well-being.

Oxygen bars are even opening up in cities, instead of stopping off for a pint on the way home, people can pop in for an energy boost both physically and mentally with a quick blast of pure oxygen. I'm still an advocate of a couple of lagers down the pub, much better for you! Fast food and chocolate bars often contain additional nutritional supplements to make up for poor eating habits leading to mineral and vitamin deficiencies, with drop-in health kiosks popping up for on the spot advice and treatment.

Some gyms offer complete work-outs in five minutes with specially designed machines to work out the entire body.

Even relaxation has to fit into a tight schedule with five-minute massages, ten-minute floatation tank sessions, and power-napping becoming normal way to recharge and relax. This type of person does not look for a slow way to chill out at the end of the day, but a source of instant Karma.

'When it comes to the trends and which categories I feel I fit into, then it would have to be a combination of 'Quick living' and 'Air of tranquillity'. I do lead a busy life where time is of the essence but I also enjoy escaping from it all and, like everyone else, dream of a quieter, more natural way of life.'

design basics

At one time, a home had the practical function of being a place to live, and there was not much difference between one home and another. Now, more than ever, a home and garden express who we are as people, telling ourselves, and others, what kind of life we lead. People are becoming far more design-aware, and the boom in the home improvement market means that new 'designer' products are becoming more available, more cheaply than ever. We spend hours looking through magazines and shops, watching TV shows about how to improve our interiors. The same amount of thought needs to go into designing your garden. A well-designed garden enables you to enjoy the space outdoors, and it can also act as an extension to the home.

Like an interior, it is important that a garden should be a functional space that fulfils your requirements. There are many considerations to take into account, and every site is different in size, shape, soil type, aspect or location. Balancing practical considerations with an attractive appearance is vital. This probably sounds a bit daunting but the following section will guide you through the process. I think it helps to remember that a 'designed garden' can often look a little staged to start with, but over the years you can develop it by adding and removing items, so it changes as you and your requirements change.

The design process

A garden should be a space that extends your home and provides you with a place to escape from the demands of life. But before you start designing your garden you need to consider the character of your particular site, including things such as the style of your house, inside and out, the views, and the 'feel' of the spaces enclosed by the house and garden. A garden should be an expression of both the spirit of the place – that quality that makes one place different from the next – and your personality, much as the interior of your house does. Some designers can be quite rigid about how a garden should blend with the architecture and the landscape in which it is situated, that all gardens should be historical masterpieces made to fit the era of your home. You do need to be aware of your surroundings, of course. If you live in a thatched country cottage you don't want to design a minimalist garden using sheet steel, glass and palm trees. The real point is that we should respect the existing design without being held down by it. But there are situations where a conflict in styles can be incredibly effective. It might seem impossible to do anything interesting with a Victorian house in an urban location. And yet if you look to your surroundings for inspiration you will see all sorts of modern structures and materials which will, if used sympathetically, work well in a contemporary garden.

A rough sketch

Elements that make a garden beautiful, or not, are not just the features contained within its

'A well-designed garden enables you to enjoy the space outdoors, and it can also act as an extension to the home.'

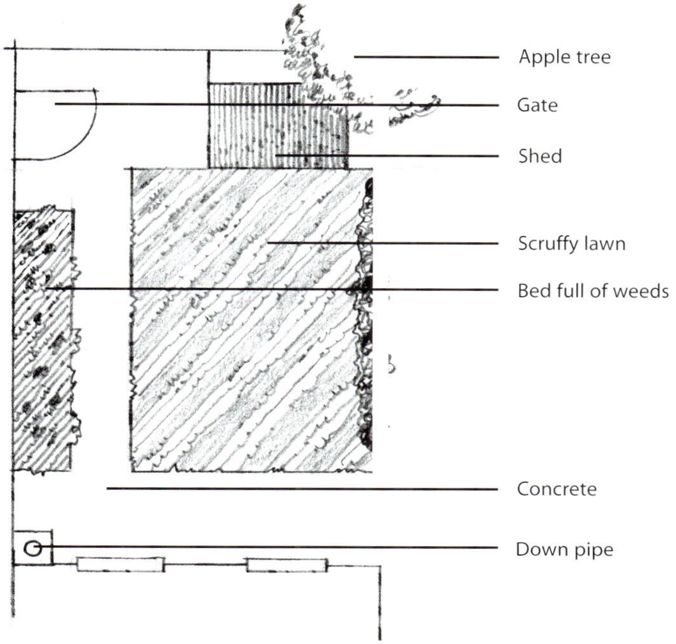

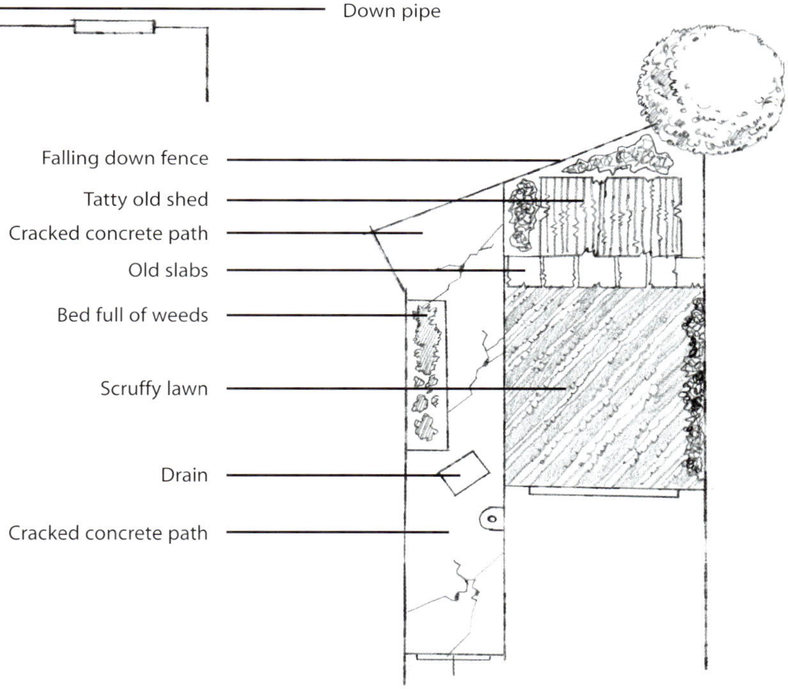

boundaries. You will need to note on the sketch any views that you wish to focus on, such as a beautiful building or a sea view, or those you need to hide, such as a factory in the distance. Also note if there are any windows over-looking your garden from neighbouring houses – you will want to block the sight of those.

Next you will need to note the lay of the land, using arrows to indicate the direction of the slope. Are there any sloping areas which may need a change of level? Are there areas needing to be back-filled to get level ground? You should also note all the existing plants and their position on the sketch plan. If there are too many, just note

The design process begins with you in the garden with a pen and a bit of paper. Make a rough sketch of the dimensions of the garden by pacing out the boundaries. Then indicate which direction your garden faces on the sketch, as this will show you where shade will fall and which areas get the most sun. Being able to see this on paper will help you decide the general positioning of all the elements in your garden, from a seating area in the sunniest places to the ideal positions for various plants, and remember that buildings and large features such as trees will cast shadows, which also need to be taken into account. Include the position of your house on your drawing, too, and include doors which provide access and windows which give you a view onto the garden.

the main plants on the sketch and write a separate list, noting the ones you wish to keep. This may influence your plans for the uses of the areas in the final design.

Finally, take a soil test to find out what type of soil you have and its pH level. This should be done at several points throughout the garden to get an overall picture of the soil. It will tell you what plants will be happy in the growing conditions in your garden. Also, take a look around you and note any plants that are growing well in your surrounding area, because this is a good indication of what plants will be suited to your space.

Once you have done these things you will be far more familiar with the space. Most importantly, you will gain a sense of how the space makes you feel. Does it make you feel exposed, or frustrated? Do you feel watched, or even claustrophobic? Note down these feelings. They will have to be addressed in the design. As you gather all this information, you will already have started the process of designing your garden.

Putting pen to paper

A great way to make a proper start on designing your garden is to establish a functional diagram of where certain features need to be located. Put out of your head any ideas of plants and materials and start to think in terms of shapes and patterns and their relationships with each other. On the diagram, just write where the main features of the garden will be situated. For example: the terrace at the sunny end, the shed in the shady area with a screen to mask it. Do you want a play area for kids, a pool, a pond or a greenhouse?

One fundamental mistake many people make when designing gardens is to try to squeeze as much as they can into the space. You have to be very selective and prioritise which are the most important elements for you. As with most areas of design, the best ideas are often the simplest; cluttering and overcrowding a space will only make it feel small and uninviting. So finding out what you need from the space is of more importance than its aesthetic qualities, and only once this is sorted out can you start thinking about features and plants.

A successful garden design should not make you feel exposed or too enclosed. Often when you go into a garden you will get either a sense of being cramped by over-planted beds (Masses), or find the opposite sensation, where it is just a great expanse of fence-to-fence lawn (Voids). Both feel uncomfortable. Masses are the structures and planting beds, and Voids are empty spaces, such as paving, paths and lawns, through which people move. A well-designed garden will have a balance between Masses and Voids.

'You should also note all the existing plants and their position on the sketch plan. If there are too many, just note the main plants on the sketch and write a separate list, noting the ones you wish to keep. This may influence your plans for the uses of the areas in the final design.'

Choosing a style

The style of your garden should say as much about you as the style of your house. We spend ages deciding on a style or theme for our interiors, and the same decision process should be involved in the garden. The beauty with gardens (much like people) is that they are hugely varied and full of almost infinite possibilities. If you as a person yearn for order and structure in your life and have little time for leisure, an informal plant lover's garden will probably not be for you, whereas a low maintenance, 'easy garden', using straight lines and a sense of minimalism, may be right up your street. It can help to see your style preferences as pairs of opposites: informal or formal; modern or traditional. But you can mix them up to create striking effects. A traditional Victorian town house can be gutted and turned into an open-plan, modern, designer home. If it is done well, the mix of old with new can be very effective.

A formal style of garden will give the space a strong sense of order. The use of geometry in the design will provide a feeling of calm through the sense that everything is in its place. In fact, gardens are generally a way of controlling Mother Nature, and this style of garden will give you that feeling of order and security from the less controllable elements of life. Of course, this will appeal to certain types of people; others will want its opposite, an informal space.

Informal gardens create a sense of natural calm, totally different to the formal garden. They feel as if they have simply grown by being lived in, with little effort from you. But in reality this is just an illusion. True, this style of garden demands less attention, and it will evolve in a more natural way than the formal garden, but to design an informal garden demands as much attention to detail as a formal one does. Maybe even more. In all gardens, you are taming and controlling the natural elements for a desired effect. But in the case of an informal garden, the atmosphere doesn't feel created at all. An informal garden will suit people that don't mind a sense of disorder and a garden that has an apparent lack of control.

It is also possible to mix the formal with the informal. Formality works well when near the house, which is a formal object. But as you move away from the house, a sense of informality will act as an interesting contrast and create a journey full of interest.

At the end of the day, a garden has to say something about what you like in terms of colours, style, use and your life, so these rules are only a guide. In fact, I hate the term 'rules': a garden should be a creative juxtaposition of elements mixed in any way that suits you, as long as the space feels balanced and pleasing to all that spend time there. If it does, then you've done a good job.

Geometry in design

Geometry – lines and shapes – is the basis on which you design gardens. When using hard landscaping and plants, you essentially use the same elements you would to make a garden, because these elements create three-dimensional spaces that people can sit in, walk through and enjoy. Hard landscaping creates hard geometric lines on or near the ground, and together these lines create patterns. Becoming aware of the effect these different patterns can have will give you the basic knowledge of how to use them deliberately to create gardens.

Different shapes and patterns have different visual effects. Shapes such as circles, squares, hexagons and octagons are all static shapes, and they are ideal for sitting areas, or areas to stop and relax on your way through the space. This is because they are of equal proportions and there is no feeling of a need to go anywhere. When surrounded by planting, they create a very intimate space.

More motive shapes, such as long thin rectangles, ovals, and patterns with flowing curves, all draw the eye through a space. This is especially true of straight lines. Motive shapes create a sense of fast movement.

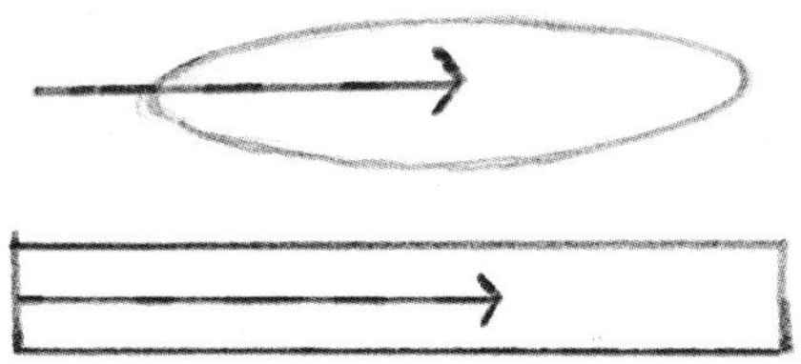

You need to be very careful when using long thin lines through the garden; you are much better off using strong bold shapes that make a gentle flowing movement through the space.

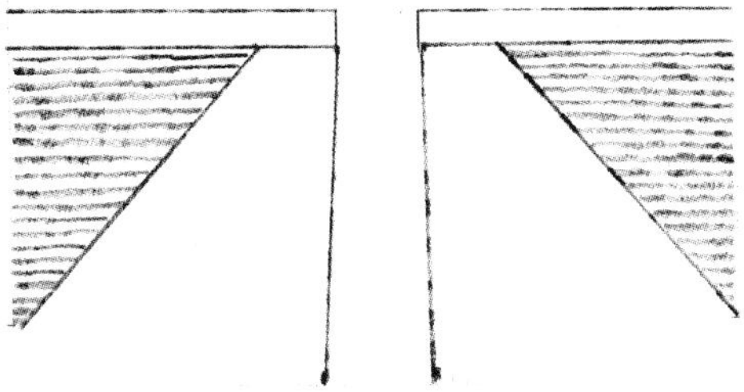

Long straight lines lead the eye and make the space feel long and thin, which is normally not attractive. The shapes created by these lines don't usually have any visual interest.

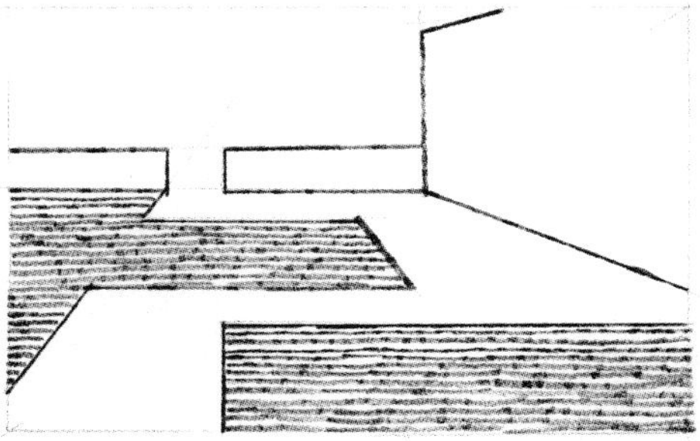

With strong lateral lines, on the other hand, the eye moves gently through the space and the shapes created are far more visually stimulating.

Another great way to create interest and movement through a space is to use a plan based on squares and rectangles all at 45 degrees to each other.

This creates a slower movement through the space, and a sense of anticipation: 'What's around the corner?' This method is also ideal for thin gardens that you want to make feel wider. It is a good example of how, by using a combination of static and motive spaces, you can create a garden with lots of interest. There are paths leading around the space with different areas to 'stop' on the way, where you could have, for example, seating areas, a pond, or even your jacuzzi.

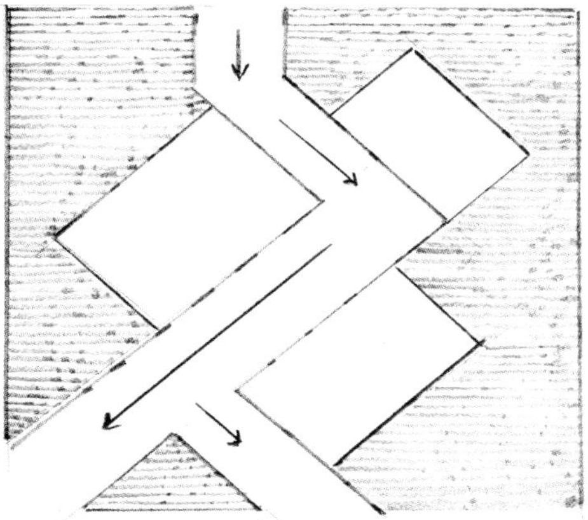

Designing using a grid

Because gardens are usually sited near a house or some kind of building, it is vital that the architecture and garden harmonise with each other. A sure-fire method of ensuring this is to use the grid method when designing your garden. The grid itself will take its lines from a major feature of the house. Using this method will automatically link the garden space with the architecture. It is one of the simplest and most effective routes to take when you are designing a garden.

Stand in the garden looking at your house and look for a feature that stands out from the rest. Look for bays, doors, and windows (which may be equally spaced), or anything else architectural that could form the basis of the grid.

The grid squares can be as large or small as you want. But my tip is that too small a grid could lead to a fussy and over-complex design. It's better to start with a larger grid and then divide it up if you need to later.

'It can help to see your style preferences as pairs of opposites: informal or formal; modern or traditional. But you can mix them up to create striking effects. A traditional Victorian town house can be gutted and turned into an open-plan, modern, designer home. If it is done well, the mix of old with new can be very effective.'

The rule of thirds

From an ancient technique known as the Golden section, used by the Greeks, and going at least as far back as the Egyptians, comes one of the most useful rules of design. A simple version of this is called the 'rule of thirds'. If you look at most houses the proportions will usually be that the roof will be 1/3 and the rest of the house will be 2/3.

This creates a feeling of balance and can be used as a simple guide to deciding on the proportions in a design. If you have a long thin plot, dividing the space into two or three sections will always work spatially and be visually pleasing.

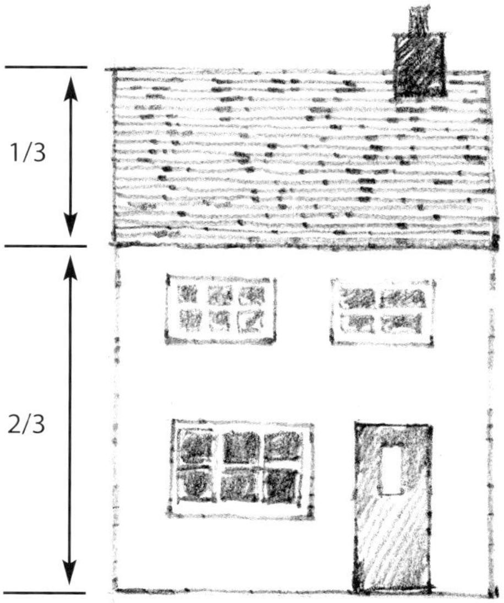

Linking home and garden

Often the easiest and most effective way to design a garden is to take inspiration from the architecture. When you have a scale drawing of the garden with the house on it, draw lines from all the windows, doors and architectural features out into the garden and use those as the dominant lines for paths, terraces, features and planting. You will see this method of design if you look at grand old houses with very formal gardens that link the house and garden visually. This method will also work with most other styles of garden, from the traditional to the very modern. Using the features of a building helps to bring a sense of unity to the design. For example, if you want a patio by the single-storey kitchen extension, you measure the height and width of this extension and translate that onto the horizontal plane. This will be the ideal size for a terrace, which will have a good visual relationship with the architecture.

The final design

Once you have decided what elements you are going to put in your garden, it is time to start the final design. Measure the garden, all the boundaries, features and their positions, and make yourself a scale drawing. It is quite simple to do this. First choose a scale (1:50 where 2 cm represent 1 metre, or 1:100 where 1 cm represents 1 metre are most common), then draw in the garden boundaries. Next, include any existing features you would like to keep in your design, such as trees. You should also draw in the position of the house and its features, such as windows and doors, and finally note which direction is north by using a compass, or just note where the sun rises and sets. You may find it easier to do it on squared or graph paper. Make loads of copies so you can try out different ideas. It is vital that you find out and mark on the plan where any services are running under the garden, such as gas, electricity, water, waste, and telephone. A friend of mine was working on a gardening programme and went through the gas main with a pick axe, and the whole cul-de-sac had to be evacuated until they fixed it.

It is important to think about routes through the garden, so make sure you link all entrances into and out of the space. If you are going to include structures such as sheds and greenhouses, you need to be sure that you can get access to them. Next, position all the areas you are going to include, such as the patio, lawn, borders, and so on. Look over the relationship between all the shapes you are putting onto paper. If they look balanced on the page, then they will probably look good when transferred to the garden for real. Once you have come up with a plan you are happy with, you need to mark it out in the garden itself. It is best to use a line marker and you may find that you change things along the way. I almost always find when I'm marking up a job that things change when they are transfered from paper to the real garden, so be prepared to move things slightly: make the path wider, move the border a touch. It will all help to create a more pleasing space. Once it is marked up, leave it for a couple of days to make sure you are happy. Look at it from an upstairs window and make sure that the sun hits the spots you intended. Then when you are happy with it, draw up a final scale plan which will help you not to order too much or too little material. You want the right number of square metres of turf for the lawn.

The lay of the land will be very influential on the design. If you have

a sloping garden, or one that has lumps and dips, then it is always good to incorporate this into the design. So don't rush in and level the whole area. You might use such features to create changing levels and ponds. Changes in level will add interest to any garden and open up a world of possibilities. It's true that a level area is far easier to design and build, and a sloping site poses design issues such as the need to level and terrace certain areas; but if treated cleverly you can use the uneven landscape to make a diverse space full of surprises. Changes in level can create ideas for interesting pathways and steps up or down through the space. Don't feel you have to walk straight up or down: have a series of steps, stopping off on the way with planted areas, hard landscaping, and exciting features. Another great way to sort out steeper slopes is to terrace them with retaining walls, which sleepers are ideal for. Terraced gardens will look great if planted with Mediterranean plants and mulched with gravel in a sunny, well-drained spot. If you have a shady garden, you could try woodland plants.

The shapes you decide on are entirely up to you. Curves will give a gentle flowing look, whereas straight lines will be more formal and lead to a design with a more structured feel. You need to be practical, too. So, for example, avoid acute angles and tight curves anywhere in the garden that there are to be borders, since it will make these parts awkward to plant.

Soil

The most important element in a garden is the quality of the soil. Good soil will mean healthy plants, so poor soil will need to be improved. Adding mulch or compost, such as worm compost (known as Gardener's Gold), which is cheap and easy to fork in, is an effective way to add high-grade organic nutrients to improve the soil. Soil is judged in terms of structure and texture. Basically all you really need to know is whether the soil you have is clay or sand, and whether it is acid or alkaline. Clay soil will be really heavy when wet. If you roll a moist ball of soil in your hand, it will smear between your thumb and forefinger and feel slightly soapy. Clay soil retains water well and is also usually quite fertile, but it can become rock hard during the summer and will need digging over with plenty of organic matter added during the winter to help improve the structure and break up the lumps. Sandy soil is easy to work. If you do the ball test in your hand and smear it between your fingers it will feel gritty and sandy. It doesn't retain water well, which means the nutrients get leached out, so it will need plenty of organic matter added regularly to maintain a fertile soil. You should do an acid test to find out whether you have an acid or alkaline soil, since this will determine what type of plants are suitable for your garden. You can buy cheap testing kits in garden centres. Try and get a liquid tester kit. I find these work much better than the metal probe type. Test the garden in various different areas because the pH level can vary throughout a site. The pH scale goes from 1–14. A neutral soil is the ideal and will read pH 7. Anything above this will be on the alkaline side, and anything below will be acid. If you have a reading of between 6.5 and 7.5, then pretty much any plant will be fine. A lower reading and you will be able to grow rhododendrons, acers and camellias, for example. If it is above 7, then you can plant things like Venetian sumach (Cotinus coggygria), Mock orange (Philadelphus), and Coneflower (Rudbeckia). You can create raised beds or have pots with specific soils, if you need a more acid or alkiline soil to plant something in particular, but it is almost impossible to change the soil pH in the whole garden. The best option is to choose plants that are suited to the soil you have. There are plenty to suit all different soils, so you'll never be short of choice.

Other factors determining what will grow in your garden are the climate and microclimate. The climate is based on factors such as rain fall, average temperature, wind and the extremes in temperature, all of which will affect the growing conditions. Climatic conditions will vary through the country, and will be affected by local geography, altitude, hills, mountains and masses of water. Each garden will have its own microclimate, as well, which is the result of any buildings which surround it, and things like fences, hedges and trees. Cities are warmer than the surrounding countryside and you very rarely get frosts. This will mean a greater choice of tender exotics and plants that wouldn't survive without winter protection in a more exposed site.

You cannot change the climate but you can manipulate the microclimate. For example, if you live in an area exposed to strong winds, you can install a wind break. This might be a simple screen, or you might plant a group of trees and shrubs that will filter out winds and create a far more hospitable microclimate for your plants and for you! A word of warning though. If you build a solid barrier, such as a brick wall, it will add to your problems, for wind will jump over the top and a swirling effect will result. A good wind break should filter wind. Planted screens or woven fences are best.

Other buildings will also affect the microclimate in your garden. Buildings will channel winds between them, and act as barriers to the sun and the rain. Sun and shade in your space will need to be considered carefully in terms of planting and seating areas. Be aware that any building will create areas where rain will not hit the soil, so you will get areas that will be extremely dry, especially at the base of walls. Keep an eye on these areas and plant a good distance away from the base of walls.

You may also get frost pockets in your garden. These result when cold air sits at the lowest points in the garden, or at the base of solid walls and fences. Choose plants that are frost hardy for these areas and remove solid barriers, replacing them with boundaries that allow free air flow. This will keep cool air moving and limit frost.

the lifescapes

the socialising garden

This is the garden for people who love people; it could be for large extended families who like to get together for long, lazy summer lunches, mid-week barbecues, or Bonfire Night mayhem. It will be the perfect garden for young people who live to party or the family with teenagers who make it an open house for their friends. It is certainly for the type of people who say 'let's go back to our place' at the drop of a hat.

A versatile space

This garden will be versatile enough to accommodate any type of get together, whether spontaneous or carefully planned. All the essentials are in place – lighting for atmosphere, hidden speakers to pump out tunes, beer and wine chillers, and heaters carefully placed so the party doesn't have to move inside when the temperature drops. Space for outdoor cooking, eating and drinking are obviously essential, but why not create a space for dancing too? There are more secluded corners for quieter occasions, for conversation (or romance!) away from the main event, and one or two dramatic features will act as conversation ice-breakers and give the garden focus. Everything contributes to hospitality, from the design of the space to the herbs specially grown for the barbecue marinades. Planting, pathways, and landscaping will all be robust because it goes without saying this garden will see plenty of action!

Designing an outdoor dining area

Dining outside has a far more celebratory feel than meat and two veg on your lap in front of the telly. I swear the food tastes better outdoors. Be it during the day or under a starry sky, the 'al fresco' atmosphere beats the dining room hands down. When designing

'Dining outside has a far more celebratory feel than the usual meat and two veg on your lap in front of the telly, I swear the food tastes better.'

this area of the garden there are a number things to think about. Firstly, should it be in the sun or in the shade? Nowadays, with the much stronger summer sun, more people are choosing shade over sun, especially if they are having a party during the day (which no doubt will last all day!). The shade of a tree may be enough, but if you don't have the space or time to wait for one to grow then a pergola with climbers, a retractable awning, or even a sail cloth stretched between scaffolding poles, will serve well. Then you need to ensure that you have enough space to fit the hordes of people that will be dropping in on you. A patio or decked area will need to be at least 3 metres by 3 metres, which is only really enough room for a table of four – so if you have the space make it bigger. Ensure there is enough room for people to fit without feeling squashed in. You will need a work area for food preparation, which will take up quite a bit of space. Have this area in a sheltered spot and out the way of the wind so your guests don't get smoked out.

Garden furniture can play a major visual and practical role in the space, so consider carefully when choosing it. From style to materials, all will affect how well the pieces work. Wood will need treating. Sculptural seating needs to be comfy. Do you want moveable or fitted furniture?

The ideal is to have something like a fitted kitchen for the outdoors, with a barbecue, solid surfaces, and shelves all in the same area. I'm still an advocate of the fitted barbecue instead of those cumbersome gas-powered things that don't really look nice. And make sure that cooking surface is big enough for at least ten large steaks! The area itself should be as near to the house as possible, and ideally near the kitchen too because the last thing you'll want is to be running back and forth to the kitchen, rather than spending time with your guests. If you have the space, you should try to provide areas away from the main party for more intimate moments, or for a quiet chat. An arbour, or any other kind of cosy area will work well.

Garden furniture

There are loads of different styles of garden furniture available, from cast iron and traditional-looking, to sleek pieces that are works of art as well as

furniture. There are also very different price brackets. You can get cheaper stuff in your local house-and-garden superstore, or a designed piece made especially for your space. You could even make improvised seating from reclaimed or found materials. You just have to make sure that the items you choose are complementary to the space. Plastic, moulded chairs have no place in a minimalist, formal space, but clean, simple, fitted stone benches would be suitable. I know this seems obvious, but you'd be surprised at some of the things you see in gardens.

Other types of seating

You will want as much seating as you can accommodate in the space, and there are clever ways of providing this. Any change of level can be treated as seating. Low walls and raised beds can be turned into seats simply by attaching chunky timber tops like a coping. For a formal entertaining area use permanent fitted furniture. You could even try concrete, which is amazingly diverse and can be poured into almost any shape. Ground stone can be added to simulate natural stone, and concrete can be dyed, textured, or even polished, to give it a really contemporary look. What I've done in my garden is to build simple benches with the same timber as I have on my deck. Their simple rectangles fit the contemporary style of the garden. I have also used strips of frosted glass on all sides of my deck and along the side return to the house, making as much use of the small space as possible. The glass is illuminated from the inside, creating a soft glow and a serene atmosphere in the evenings.

> 'Concrete is truly diverse and can be poured into almost any shape. Ground stone can be added to simulate natural stone or it can be dyed, textured, or even polished for a really contemporary look.'

Choosing materials

Of course you will need a table or two, and the bigger the better, since when you eat outdoors you seem to end up with far more stuff on the table – salads, garlic bread, all the meat, wine, condiments, glasses, etc. It is most important to be sure the table is on a level surface, because there is nothing more annoying that a rocking table – not very relaxing at all! So choose a material that is solid under foot and without too many lumps and bumps. Gravel is not the best; lawn can work well, if you make sure that it is good and level, but beware that if you leave anything on the lawn for long periods, you will end up with patches that die back and turn yellow and brown, so move any furniture after use. The best

options are paved areas, decks, resin-bonded gravel or tiling, all of which offer everything you need: a flat, solid area – the ideal for a dining area. Granted it can cost quite a bit to lay such a space, so if your budget won't stretch that far you can get away with gravel instead. Just make sure the ground is well compacted, preferably with hardcore, or hoggin, underneath to help with drainage and give it a more solid base. If you do this you can always pave over the top at a later date, when you can afford it.

'Planting will need to be pretty robust and be able to cope with a bit of neglect, because with all these parties Sunday mornings will be for sleeping off hangovers rather than gardening, or you just won't have the time of course. Just avoid anything that needs regular pruning such as roses and clipped box, and use evergreen shrubs at the back of the borders to provide a backdrop for other plants.'

The lighting

Lighting will play a major role in creating atmosphere for evening parties. There are a vast array of different products on the market, from the relatively cheap to the more complex systems designed specifically for your space. I always use oil burners when we have people over in the summer. I found some really cheap ones in a local garden centre for less than a fiver each, and I've got about six of them placed amongst planting and by seating areas. The flickering naked flames create a fantastic mood. It will be important to have lighting so that people can find their way around the space (especially after one too many), so illuminate steps, pathways, and all areas of access. If you have a pond, make sure it's lit too (I've ended up in an unlit pond before, very funny, but very wet!). Don't overdo it though. The last thing you want is a home version of the Blackpool illuminations that can be seen for miles around. Coloured lighting is something that I find people are a little scared of, but the effects you can produce can be amazing. I met with a chap the other week who has developed an LED light that changes colour slowly. He also had LED strip lights, spot lights, all sorts of cool stuff, in his garden. When you direct and blend lights of different colours, you can create great effects. However, it is important to pick out a few elements in the garden that you want to have as focal points – perhaps a feature plant or a sculpture. Dot the odd light amongst planting, play with shadows, light and dark and silhouettes, and spend a bit of time fiddling with lights until you create the effect you are after. I also have just had a fader fitted to some of the lights in my garden, which offers an even better sense of control and atmosphere.

The planting

Planting will need to be pretty robust and able to cope with a bit of neglect, because with all these parties Sunday mornings will be for sleeping and

recovering rather than gardening. Just avoid anything that needs regular pruning, such as roses and clipped box, and use evergreen shrubs at the back of the borders to provide a backdrop for other plants. Try not to use too many perennials that will need cutting back and dividing, and don't use plants that will need winter protection. Of course, this all depends on experience and time, and on your interest in learning a bit more about plants and planting. So ask questions at the garden centre and take their advice on which plants to use. As with any garden, a sense of privacy helps create the sense of escapism that you want to experience, so the last thing you want is to feel that people are watching you. If you can create a garden that is surrounded with abundant borders then not only will you feel more secluded, but any noise created by any gathering you have is more likely to be filtered by the living sound-proofing that you have planted.

Planting list

Bamboos
Camellia
Choisya ternata
Euphorbia
Ferns
Geranium 'Johnson's Blue'
Hostas
Lavender
Magnolia
Mahonia
Palms
Phormium
Santolina
Skimmia japonica
Stachys byzantina
Viburnum tinus

Geranium 'Johnson's Blue'

Euphorbia Characias

the sanctuary garden

The sanctuary garden is for anyone who wants a tranquil place to escape to in the midst of a hectic life. It's for those who feel stressed and want a space to put life and its demands back into perspective. It might simply be a secluded corner in the family garden that a busy mum can call her own and use to recharge and relax in. The sanctuary garden is simple, and is designed to help you wind down and restore balance to mind, body, and soul.

A sanctuary garden is your safe haven; a refuge offering a total escape from the world. It should be a garden with secret places and nooks that offer sun or shade. Everything about it relaxes the mind and restores the spirit. Pathways meander gently through lush planting to absorb noise and pollution. The sounds here are muted and soothing – running water, footsteps on gravel. Colours and lighting are soft and subtle. The plants provide relaxing aromas to soothe the soul.

Creating secluded boundaries

A sanctuary cannot be achieved without a sense of seclusion. Most gardens are already enclosed by fences or, if you're really lucky, trees and hedges. Typically, however, fences are harsh, bland expanses of plain timber that provide no sense of calm whatsoever. It is therefore vital to design your garden in such a way that all the boundaries are covered with planting to create a soothing sense of seclusion. Being surrounded by calming green foliage will instantly begin to help create your 'sanctuary'.

'A problem that many people have, especially in small town gardens, is prying eyes from overlooking windows – how can you have a true sanctuary if people are able to see you?'

A problem that many people have, especially in smaller town gardens, is prying eyes from overlooking windows. How can you have a true sanctuary if people are able to see you? Remember that your garden is also influenced by things beyond its boundary. When you start to design your garden, it's a good idea to stand in the middle of it and make a list of all the views you want to block and all the views you wish to make the most of. If you have a great view of a valley, a lake, or even the London Eye, you will want to preserve this view, so it's no good planting a tree or building a tea hut somewhere that will obscure it. On the other hand, if what you see are neighbours' windows

A garden in its very essence is a sanctuary – a space for the imagination, display, relaxation and escape. But many gardens are crying out for a small area where the owner can just chill out. Most people who want this style of garden will instantly think of feng shui and Oriental influences. Yes, the Oriental look is ideal for creating a sanctuary but it's not the only way.

In an English country garden, for example, a space of sanctuary could be created by things such as a rose-covered arbour and an ornate iron bench overlooking a pond. In an exotic garden it could be a small decked area surrounded by lush tropical planting. In the designer garden it could be an outdoor room created as a minimalist space to do yoga. Essentially, a space of sanctuary can be created in many different ways in any sort of garden.

or a power station, you immediately know where to plant trees and build the tea house.

A space of sanctuary

When planning your garden, the first thing to do is to decide whether you want your sanctuary to be a place to sit in the sun or a sheltered spot for staying cool and relaxing in. For me, the ideal is an area set in dappled shade where you can have the best of both worlds, with light and shade creating the calming impression of being in a sheltered glade or clearing. Plants will play a major role in achieving a peaceful place so avoid any that are spiky because they promote a feeling of energy. Feng shui says that spiky shaped plants should never be kept in the bedroom because they don't promote calm or a good night's sleep.

I'm not a great follower of feng shui but I agree that anything visually energetic will not create a soothing atmosphere. It's therefore best to choose plants with rounder leaves and a lush look.

'If you are going to just create one area of the garden for your sanctuary then the shape of the area will be vital, you will need to choose a shape that is of equal proportions, such as a square or a circle, because these shapes encourage you to stop and relax, whereas ovals and rectangles are motive, spaces more suited to areas which people traffic will flow.'

The shape

If you are going to dedicate just one area of the garden to being a sanctuary, the shape of the area is vital. You will need to choose a shape that is of equal proportions, such as a square or circle, because these shapes encourage you to stop and relax. Ovals and rectangles are motive and therefore more suited to areas with people traffic. Try to situate the space away from the social areas of the garden, and design your sanctuary as a reward – something to look forward to at the end of the journey through your garden.

Screening your sanctuary

It's best if your sanctuary area can't be seen from the main areas of the garden. Screening is therefore vital, and there are a number of methods you can use to achieve it. You can create seclusion by planting things in a certain way. A tree or a number of trees make a fantastic basis for a sanctuary. If you already have a tree in your garden, then all the better. If not, try to choose a suitable one for the size of your garden, and be sure to choose one with quite a loose canopy such as Silver birch *(Betula pendula)*. *Betula* cast beautiful shadows that dance around the garden throughout the day. You could even combine a *Betula* with a tree seat or hammock to create a very simple sanctuary. Surrounding an area with

a mixture of evergreen shrubs, aromatic plants, and soft coloured flowering plants is another great way to create a secluded area. If you use a large evergreen shrub to block views from the main garden, it will add more to the sense of privacy. Trellis screens planted with climbers will also act as successful screens and create private areas.

The Oriental style

The Oriental style works particularly well in this type of garden and has been a major influence on garden design. In Japanese gardens, simplicity creates a sense of calm, which works especially well in a small space. The Japanese garden strives for affinity with natural things, so all the materials look natural and are used in a simple way. The planting aims for the same effect and tries to create an entire landscape in miniature, where rocks represent mountains, and clipped trees and hedges represent clouds. There is raked gravel and flowing water. Water plays an important role in achieving calm in the garden and is always presented in a gentle manner: either as a trickling stream or a still pool. There is a feeling of serenity in such gardens and the gentle noise of the water soothes the mind. You could also install outdoor speakers so you can listen to relaxation CDs in the garden to add to the relaxing atmosphere. Other features you might find in the Japanese garden are lanterns, bridges, smooth stepping stones, tea houses, and meandering paths, with places along the way to stop and appreciate the garden.

Now personally, I believe that trying to create a Japanese garden in the context of a suburban garden will almost always look fake and out of place. What I would suggest instead is to borrow elements from its design and adapt them to suit your own sanctuary. To create a defined space, find something to grow climbers over such as *Wisteria sinensis*. Its beautiful, over-hanging, fragrant flowers create a really restful space. You could also use a pergola with trellis on the sides to create green walls. Planting bamboo around the space will add a sense of height and the old cliché, 'movement', with the sound of leaves rustling in the cool breeze. Walking on stepping stones through lush planting would be perfect and would add a sense of discovery and intrigue. Just imagine the scene: tall bamboos, big-leaved Japanese aralia (*Fatsia japonica*), plaintain lillies *(hostas)*, and then, there in the clearing, is the sanctuary. I can picture it all so well and I wish I had a bigger garden to play with!

'Water features can another dimension to the space and there are a number of options and combinations depending on the size of the area you have. For a small space there are hundreds of small water features available.'

Water features

Water features add another interesting dimension to the sanctuary garden and there are various options to suit the size of your space. For small spaces, there are hundreds of water features available, and what you go for will depend on your personal taste. I suggest simple, slate monoliths (where the water comes up a hole in the middle and gently trickles down the sides), spheres, or even a stainless steel column, which will not only offer the sight and sound of water, but beautiful reflections as well (especially with a light by it). In a larger garden, you can dream up far grander schemes and build a stream leading to a small waterfall dropping into a still pool. I can also picture a secluded patio, covered by a pergola cloaked with flowers and foliage – I feel relaxed just thinking about it.

A chill-out zone

The ultimate chill-out zone would have to be one with a hot tub, positioned in a totally private section of the garden, surrounded by plants – just be sure to have screens, living or not, and trees to protect you from prying eyes. Bathing au naturel in the great outdoors, enjoying a glass of champagne is about as relaxing as it gets. An outdoor building to house it would be a good idea. You may even want to install a music system, a small fridge and some lighting for those warm summer nights.

Some final thoughts

Just a few final points. The overall feel of the space in a sanctuary garden should be a calming, sensory one, with a combination of relaxing sights, sounds, and aromas. You may also wish to include plants and materials to touch: wood, natural stone, and gravel all offer

different textures and contrast well with each other. For pergolas and rooms in the garden, you can use old telegraph poles as uprights. They will provide a chunky look and a feeling of permanence, and they can also act as sturdy supports for you to string a hammock from. Green is a calming colour, so ensure the whole space is enclosed by lush planting and out of view from the rest of the garden. Include aromatic plants such as lavenders, herbs (which can be used in herbal teas), and fragrant flowers. Use lighting to create atmosphere by illuminating special plants, water features, certain focal points, and any paths leading to the area. Finally, remember that all gardens should be a sanctuary, or at least contain somewhere you can escape to, so that you can relax and forget the rest of the world.

Main elements

- Gazebo/pergola
- Hidden nooks
- Japanese style
- Seats among planting
- Woodland retreats

Colours

- Cool blue
- Green
- Lilac
- White

Optional features

- Chimes
- Hot tub
- Lighting
- Music
- Water
- Glass
- Sculpture
- Heater

Planting list

Carex
Cercis chinensis
Ceratostigma willmottianum
Chaenomeles
Cornus florida
Fargesia nitida
Gunnera manicata
Hostas
Irises
Japanese maples
Lilacs
Miscanthus sinensis 'Zebrinus'
Nandina domestica
Osmanthus x burkwoodii
Panicum
Photinia x fraserei 'Red robin'
Phyllostachys aurea
Phyllostachys nigra
Pieris japonica
Salvia
Sasa veitchii
Tricyrtis formosana
Weigela rosea

Chaenomeles

Lilac

the gardener's garden

This is the garden for people who don't just want to sit back and look – they want to get out there and do. It's for people who want to extend their knowledge about the soil, plants, and cycles of growth. They also like to enjoy the fruits of their labour. It may be for someone who has retired and now has the time to take up a new hobby, or indulge in an existing one. Or it may just be the escape needed for those of you who have some spare energy and find the discipline of planting and nurturing to be an antidote to the fast pace of everyday life. It can also be a great source of fresh-grown produce.

The gardener's garden will be designed for activity and interest throughout the year. Path networks provide easy access to all areas of the garden for planting, weeding, feeding, and harvesting. Plants are carefully chosen to create a balance between beauty and productivity, and there should be areas dedicated to vegetables and fruit bushes. This is a plant lover's garden. It's for the type of person who enjoys a challenge and, through commitment and devotion over the years, will create a fantastic display of vibrant colours, glorious scents, and abundant planting.

This is not the easiest garden in the world to design. In fact, design is not a word that is well suited to this space. It develops naturally and isn't something that can be rushed. Be prepared to make mistakes, as this is the way you will learn what works and what doesn't. Even the most experienced gardeners make mistakes – so don't worry! Every garden is individual, whether in terms of style, space, soil type, amount of light, climate, or microclimate, so you will have to work around these restrictions.

'This is not the easiest garden in the world to design; in fact design is not a word that is suited well to this space.'

Planning work areas

First, you will need to make decisions about which elements will make up your garden. Do you want a vegetable patch, fruit trees, or herbaceous borders? Where are the shed and greenhouse going to go? You will need to strike a balance between the elements of a 'working garden' and those that create a sense of beauty. Work areas will be needed, of course, but they should be screened off and positioned carefully to avoid drawing attention to them.

The garden shed

You will need a number of different gardening tools for a garden like this and so a decent-sized shed is a must-have. Most gardens will have a shady corner where it is difficult to grow things, but it makes the perfect position for a shed.Ideally, the shed should be screened from the rest of the garden since they are normally not the most beautiful structures in the world! One good way of doing this is to plant evergreen shrubs that will grow tall enough to hide it. Or you could place a trellis screen planted with climbers, preferably evergreen, in front of it. You could even grow plants over the shed. It could also be part of a dedicated work zone at the end of the garden, which is completely fenced off.

You may like to have a greenhouse for nurturing young seedlings, growing exotics, or over-wintering delicate plants. The position of your greenhouse is vitally important to the microclimate created within it, so there are a few things to keep in mind when finding a place for it in the garden. Greenhouses need light, but if they get too much direct sunlight they will become like an oven. The ideal is for the longer side of the greenhouse to run from west to east. You may want to run power to your greenhouse for lighting, heating, or perhaps a radio. Having a tap nearby is also handy. Plan to have a small area just outside the greenhouse for acclimatising plants to the outside.

A few other things to consider: a greenhouse should be placed on a solid base to ensure it remains level. Shelving maximises growing space. Providing ventilation is essential for maintaining a free flow of air within the greenhouse. For over-wintering plants, a constant temperature of 5–7 °C is needed, so consider insulating the greenhouse with bubble wrap. If it becomes too hot in the summer, you can get a wash to paint onto the glass, which protects it from the sun's hot rays.

Avoid painting your shed bright colours, which will draw attention to it. The best colours will be natural tones such as browns and dark greens.

The planting

The gardener's garden is about plants working together and creating the best use of the space available. The vegetable patch does not necessarily have to be in its own separate area at the far end of the garden. Vegetables can be combined with other plants, especially if space is limited. Just make sure you choose varieties that are attractive enough to blend in with their surroundings. For example, try planting a beautiful globe artichoke amongst your flowerbeds. It will act as an eye-catching silvery-grey feature. Or perhaps try planting fennel with its tall, feathery foliage. It provides a wonderful contrast to many different types of plant. However, you don't want to bung uninspiring potato plants amongst your flowerbeds for they are far from attractive. After all, you can easily buy huge bags of potatoes for very little down at the shops. Plant vegetables that are more unusual and not so easily available, or ones that don't taste as good as they should from the shops.

Herbs

A gardener will definitely want to include a range of herbs in the garden. Herbs work well by themselves in pots by the kitchen door, or amongst other plants in the flowering borders. The obvious choices are herbs such as rosemary, which is an attractive evergreen shrub with dainty, blue, edible flowers in the spring. Sweet bay *(Laurus nobilis)*, which is usually hardy, is easily shaped and clipped to create visual interest. If clipped into a tall column, it creates a great vertical accent. If kept in a pot, sweet bay will not tolerate harsh frosts, so it should be kept in a sheltered, frost-free environment during the winter months. A nice method of planting herbs is to position them near and around seating areas and paths, or anywhere where their aromas and attractive foliage can be appreciated. There is a huge variety of herb species, so feel free to experiment with contrasting leaf sizes, shapes, colours, and textures. For example, place purple sage mixed with chives and thyme around a large pot containing an architectural plant, such as a smaller variety of phormium. Planting herbs amongst flowering borders is ideal for a small garden, but avoid planting mint, which will spread out of control. If you must have mint, you should know that it spreads by sending out underground stems and the best way to control it is with buried tiles or in a plastic flower pot with the bottom cut off.

Plants for flower arranging

The gardener's garden is also a place for growing plants that are good for flower arranging. There is nothing better than being able to bring the sights and smells of the garden into the home. Just think how much money you could save. Flower arrangements are at their best with a mixture of foliage and flowers. A florist once told me that flowers were easy to come by but that she was always on the lookout for sources of foliage, which wasn't so easy to find and much more expensive. Most florists use eucalyptus for foliage: it grows quickly and quite happily over here, there are loads of different varieties available, and they grow very big quite rapidly. You may wish to consider them for the garden. If you cut them down to knee-height every spring, you can keep them as a smallish shrub. When a eucalyptus is cut back, it produces attractive, rounded leaves. But as it gets larger, the leaves become longer and thinner and much less appealing. Another plant that will tolerate regular cutting and is ideal for arrangements is Mexican orange blossom 'Sundance' *(Choisya ternate)*. It has aromatic foliage and leaves in pretty bunches of three. Some others to try are: *Elaeagnus x ebbingei*, spindle tree 'Silver Queen' *(Euonymus fortunei)*, *Viburnum davidii,* or silk-tassel bush *(Garrya elliptica)*. You could also try one of my favourites, *Itea ilicifolia*, which is often quite expensive in garden centres but worth every penny. Grown on a sunny wall, it will produce long green-yellow catkins that are beautiful in the garden and in flower arrangements.

Ferns

Ferns are also highly valued both in the garden and in flower arrangements. I have a whole corner dedicated to ferns in my garden and it is my favourite corner. Good ferns to try are Buckler

fern *(Dryopteris)* or Shield fern *(Polystichum)*. Grasses can also look great and there are loads to choose from; among my favourites are Fountain grass *(Pennisetum)* and Crab grass *(Panicum)*.

Perennials

Creating a display of flowers to last over many years in the garden is a must, so grow lots of perennials such as delphiniums, lupins, lobelia, and aquilegias. They will spread and increase in numbers and produce more flowers over time. There are so many flowers to choose from that I will just give you a list of suggestions for you to try:

Anemones
Campanulas
Dahlias
Gypsophila
Hellebores
Irises
Lilies
Michaelmas daisies *(Asters)*
Peonies
Peruvian lilies *(Alstroemeria)*
Roses
Sweet peas

'Ferns are also highly valued both in the garden and for flower arranging. I have a whole corner dedicated to ferns in my garden and it is my favourite corner of the garden; try *Dryopteris*, or *Polystichum*. Grasses can also look great and there are loads you could use; among my favourites are *Pennisetum* and *Panicum*.'

Plants for drying

During winter you will still want to enjoy flower arrangements, so think about growing plants that can be dried and used for this purpose. The easiest way to dry plants is to pick them when they have no moisture on them (on a sunny day) and tie them in small bunches and hang them upside down to let them dry out. Or you can use silica gel, which absorbs moisture, and seal them in a container for two or three days. There are lots of things you could try to dry, such as delphiniums, foxgloves, poppies, *Achillea*, globe thistles *(Echinops)*, sea holly *(Eryngium)*, lavender, love-in-the-mist, and sunflowers. All work well, but, really, give anything a chance and it may work too!

Choosing materials

The hard materials you choose for this garden will need to reflect the loose, natural appearance of the space. Brick pathways winding their way around the garden are the ideal choice, but if that proves too expensive just edge the paths with brick and then chuck down some gravel. For gardeners who find it a struggle to bend down to weed and plant, or who are confined to a wheel-chair, raised beds are ideal. However, make sure the beds are no wider than your reach to ensure access to all the plants. Raised beds also help to create interesting levels within a garden. They can be constructed using bricks, stone, or timber. New railway sleepers are ideal for raised beds, steps, and terracing, but be aware that old sleepers can leach out carcinogenic chemicals and should not be used, especially near vegetable patches and other food crops; buy new ones, which are usually around £25 each. Paved areas will look great in brick with herringbone or basket-weave patterns. Or use real stone paving like

Yorkstone or one of the great imitation concrete pavers that are now available. You may wish to add a pergola to the garden to provide a sheltered area for seating, or to act as an interesting walk-through feature and frame an attractive view. There are lots of options open to you, from ready-made timber kits to pre-fabricated tubular metal ones. Or you could simply make one yourself. Plants such as roses, honeysuckle, and laburnum can be grown over these structures to add interest and beauty. Carefully placed 'found' items such as old gardening tools, butler sinks, and terracotta pots will give the garden an established feel. A garden is a great way of showing off your own personal style, so don't be afraid to be original. I once used an old Victorian fireplace in a garden and, framed by plants, it created a stunning effect. Having items that you don't usually see in a garden creates a quirky look.

Compost

Any real gardener will want to make compost. Compost is vital for growing plants because it enriches the soil with nutrients and improves soil structure. Kitchen and garden waste will all eventually rot down into a great compost and provide an invaluable source of nutrients and soil conditioners. You can buy ready-made compost makers or simply make one yourself out of timber. Just make sure that the compost maker is well aerated by leaving gaps in the timbers. You will also need to mix the contents occasionally, because the centre of the compost will heat up more quickly and therefore rot quicker than the rest. If the heap dries up, sprinkle it with some water. This will encourage bacteria to grow and help it to rot. Finally, be sure you cover the top to prevent either moisture-loss or too much rain getting in.

Planting list

Achillea
Allium giganteum
Alstroemeria
Anemones
Apples
Asters
Beetroot
Cabbage
Campanulas
Carrots
Courgettes
Dahlias
Echinops
Elaeagnus x ebbingei
Eryngium
Euonymus fortunei
Fennel
Foxgloves
Garlic
Garrya elliptica
Gypsophila
Hellebores
Heuchera
Irises
Itea ilicifolia
Lavenders
Leeks
Lilac
Lilies
Lupins
Peonies
Pinks
Poppies
Radishes
Rhubarb
Roses
Runner beans
Santolina
Stachys byzantina
Sweet peas
Viburnum davidii

Lupins

Achillea

the wildlife garden

The wildlife garden is about more than plants and design, and it will appeal to a wide range of people. It's a natural choice for the bird-watcher, bee-keeper, or butterfly enthusiast, and it's ideal for the family with young kids that wants an educational space to provide a close-up view of the lives of squirrels, badgers, newts, and frogs. The active-retired will enjoy it since they will have the time to watch the wildlife that visits the garden and the enthusiasm to plan how to encourage them with various plants. It may even be attractive to urban professionals who want to spend time giving something back to the environment and are keen to do their bit to preserve local plants and wildlife by creating a safe habitat in a corner of the city.

Everything about this garden is designed to attract wildlife. The overall impression of the space is unstructured and wild, but it needs to be a carefully planned haven for small mammals, with heady summer scents and an array of colours to attract birds, bees, and butterflies, and perhaps a pond to attract frogs, newts, and dragonflies. Fruiting plants will be enjoyed by visitors and gardener alike. Discreet feeding and watering stations for birds and animals will encourage them to claim the garden as their own. You could create mini-hides with seating to allow you to view wildlife without disturbing their routine.

Designing a wildlife garden

First, you will need to allow uncultivated flowers, pests, and weeds to grow – they are all food sources for a variety of wildlife such as bats, ladybirds, birds, and hedgehogs. You should aim to include

'A wildlife garden suits an informal style. Avoid using straight lines, which you don't really see in nature itself, by using gentle curves and natural-looking materials.'

plants that attract insects, which in turn will attract birds and certain mammals. Evergreen and native hedges and trees will encourage birds, and densely-planted borders crammed with flowers full of scent and nectar will provide food and a hiding place for insects and small mammals. With the widespread destruction of hedgerows and other natural habitats of birds, insects, and animals in this country, it would make a great difference if there was one corner to attract wildlife in every garden.

Elements of a wildlife garden

- A wildlife garden suits an informal style. Avoid using straight lines, which you don't really see in nature itself, by using gentle curves and natural-looking materials.
- Flower-beds should be situated in sheltered sunny corners of the garden to encourage butterflies, who like the warmth and shelter from winds.
- Include a pond, which is a sure way to attract amphibians and birds. You might want to include a small hide from which to watch birds and other animals. Making a hide can be as simple as adapting a prefab shed and staining it a dark natural colour.

The main thing to remember when creating a wildlife garden is that you don't have to dedicate the whole space to it – an area at the back of the garden could be enough. Remember that you will have to become less fussy about weeds, and let the garden do its own thing. You are there just to tidy up and cut things back when they really need it. Think about the food chain. If you can encourage the insects then you will get the birds and small mammals. Provide places for them to hide and water for them to drink. Ponds will attract an enormous range of wildlife. Plant around them with plants that will hide the edges and make them blend into the landscape, and leave rocks and bits of wood near the edges so amphibians can get in and out. The best thing about a wildlife garden is that it is a natural method of pest control, with the food chain working as nature intended.

- Allow an area of the garden to become a wild area where plants are left to their own devices. This often works well where you may have tried and failed to grow border plants.
- Create a woodland glade, which will suit the natural feel of the garden and provide a home for all sorts of creatures.
- Plant a meadow with wild flowers. This doesn't have to be done in a large area, you can simply convert a lawn or an area of lawn to meadow. The easiest way of doing this is to ignore an area and not apply weed killers or mow it; all the weeds in the lawn will then grow into what they really are – 'wild flowers'. You can also buy packs of meadow seed or pot-grown wild flowers, which can be easily planted.

Birds in the garden

The sight and sound of birds in the garden can be enjoyed all year round and is most welcome and calming. To attract them, you will need to provide three main things: food, water, and shelter.

Hedges as boundaries in the garden not only 'green up' the boundaries of the garden but provide a haven for birds to shelter in. Hedges also provide birds with food, such as insects and winter berries, when food is scarce. Evergreen hedges are ideal places for birds to nest and hide during winter, and mixed native hedges are the best because they provide not only food and shelter for birds, but plenty of seasonal interest for us, with flowers, foliage, and fruits for the gardener.

To create a mixed hedge, make use of evergreen plants to make up about a third of the hedge. Holly or cherry laurel can be good, too. Choose a few plants that are prickly to deter intruders and provide a safe nesting site. Also, let some plants grow without clipping them to encourage flowers and fruit – the best ones for this are hawthorn, firethorn *(Pyracantha)*, or even the crab apple *(Malus)*.

Trees for birds

Trees not only provide structure and height for the garden but, if carefully chosen, will encourage wildlife too. The best trees are natives, which will provide homes for the greatest number of insects for birds to feast on. You should include trees to provide you with flowers and fruit for seasonal variation. There are quite a few *Malus* trees suitable for the wildlife garden: try John Downie *(Malus 'John Downie')* or, one of my favourites, the Golden Hornet *(Malus x. zumi)*, with flowers that provide an amazing display in spring and loads of fruit in autumn. Mountain ash *(Sorbus)* is popular because the fruit is very attractive to birds – they usually strip the tree bare. Others you could try include oak (if you have a massive garden), silver birch, alder, beech, ash, and the white willow *(Salix alba)*.

Feeding birds

Another way to attract birds is to put food out for them. Bird feeders and tables are ideal because they enable you to enjoy watching the birds munching what you've left for them. You should put food out from late autumn till early spring. If it stays cold beyond that, keep feeding them until any cold snap is over. Birds come to rely on the food you put out, and if you stop for even a day or two you could be risking their lives.

Have more than one feeding station to limit the competition, and try to make them inaccessible to cats and squirrels. Remember to put them in places where you'll get a good view. Try to put food out by late morning so that it's all eaten up by the time it gets dark, otherwise you may be feeding rats and foxes too.

Different birds like different foods, but you must avoid spicy food, salty food, desiccated coconut, which swells in their stomachs, and raw meat, which can be poisonous for them. Aim for a good mix of foods to cater for all types of bird.

- Peanuts appeal to many types of bird.
- Fresh coconut cut in half is good for all types of tits.
- Seeds are great for all sorts of birds.
- Fat from the grill pan mixed with scraps will please tits and robins.
- Cooked bacon rind, cereals, dried fruit, and cooked rice attract many different types of birds.
- Chopped up apples will attract thrushes.

Birdbaths

It is essential to provide birds with drinking water and a place to wash. There are loads of birdbaths on the market these days and they range from the very ornate to ones that will suit a minimalist garden. But you don't need to spend loads of money on one unless you want it to be a feature – just use an old grill pan or bin lid and the birds can clean themselves and drink from that. And remember that in winter water will soon turn to ice, so keep fresh water on tap.

Ponds

By far the best way to attract wildlife to the garden is by putting in a pond. (see the 'How To' section on ponds). Not only is it a magnet to all sorts of wildlife and insects but it also allows you to introduce a whole new range of plants – from lily pads and water irises to bog plant's which grow around the edges and make the pond blend in naturally.

A pond will encourage frogs, toads, and newts, all of which breed and spend most of their time in and around water. They can also benefit the garden by going on missions to find food such as slugs, flies, and other nasties. There is an educational benefit too: you can watch their reproductive processes in your

own garden. It's a great learning experience for kids to watch the frog's spawn develop into tadpoles and to then see the tadpoles becoming frogs.

If you want to introduce frogs and toads quickly into the garden, you may want to go to a neighbour's pond and get some spawn from it to put in your pond. (But ask your neighbour first!) It's important not to mess with the local habitat though, so only get it from ponds that are nearby and never from the wild. Amphibians also need places to hide and hibernate during the winter, and you will want them to stay in your garden: piles of logs, rocks, or stones are ideal. They will also hide in piles of old leaves and compost heaps, so be careful if you disturb these piles for some reason.

Creating a wild corner

Plant a corner of the garden with rampant plants and leave it to do its own thing. This is ideal for awkward corners where not much else will grow. Often the plants in these 'wild' areas can reduce the amount of maintenance

'Plant a corner of the garden with rampant plants and leave it to do its own thing. This is ideal for awkward corners where not much else will grow. Often the plants in these 'wild' areas can reduce the amount of maintenance you need to do in the long run and will attract wildlife.'

you need to do in the long run and will attract wildlife. Try plants such as spurge *(Euphorbia amygdaloides)*, which will spread quite fast, lesser periwinkle *(Vinca minor),* which is a really rampant ground cover plant, and brambles, which provide fruit for food. Encourage nettle patches, which offer homes to insects and places for them to lay eggs. Nettles support over forty species of wildlife, including some of our most stunning butterflies such as the larvae of the Tortoiseshell and Peacock butterflies. Over-wintering aphids also live amongst nettles. These aphids are the favourite food of ladybirds, blue tits, and other woodland birds, which feast on them in huge numbers. Nettles also produce seeds, which the birds eat. In the wild, nettles developed their sting as a defence against grazing animals, most of which steer clear of them, which makes them the perfect, safe hiding place for insects and their larvae. Nettles are one of the most important plants in the English countryside.

Creating a woodland glade

You don't have to have loads of space to create a glade in the garden. Even

a couple of trees under-planted with small shrubs and ground cover will do the trick. They create a restful feel to the garden, adding height, dappled shade and a great place for wildlife to flourish. First of all, choose a tree that has a light canopy, such as a birch, and lay out plants underneath with a variety of heights, starting with small shrubs that carry berries such as elder or holly. Then plant woodland plants such hellebores, winter-flowering aconite's, foxgloves, lily of the valley, violets, bluebells, and forget-me-nots in front of the shrubs. This will work best at the rear of the garden, away from the structured area around the house.

Borders to attract wildlife

In general, plants that attract butterflies and other insects into the garden are brightly coloured and have strong scents. Butterflies are especially attracted to plants with blue flowers, so the obvious place to start is with the butterfly bush *(Buddleia davidii)*, which can be blue, as well as white, mauve, or pink, and is irresistible to all types of butterfly. When I was a kid, I spent whole days chasing butterflies around the buddleia at my grandparent's house and it's one of my most vivid childhood memories. Sadly, the numbers of buddleia are in decline, so it's really important for people to start to plant in a way that will help the butterfly population to thrive. It would be a shame for experiences like mine to become a thing of the past. Other great flowering shrubs are *Ceanothus,* which has tight clusters of beautiful tiny blue flowers; *Viburnum x burkwoodii,* which has highly scented white flowers in the spring; and *Syringa*, commonly known as lilac, which also flowers in spring and is great because the scent is fantastic on warm spring evenings. Be sure to also include lavender which attracts butterflies, bees, and countless other insects.

Planting list

Achilleas
Alliums
Aquilegias
Buddleia davidii
Caryopteris x clandonensis
Ceanothus
Digitalis
Hawthorn
Hyssopus officinalis
Ilex x altaclerensis 'Golden King'
Lavenders
Lonicera
Love-in-the-mist
Monarda
Pyracanthas
Sorbus aria
Viburnum opulus

Hyssopus officianalis

Monarda

the easy garden

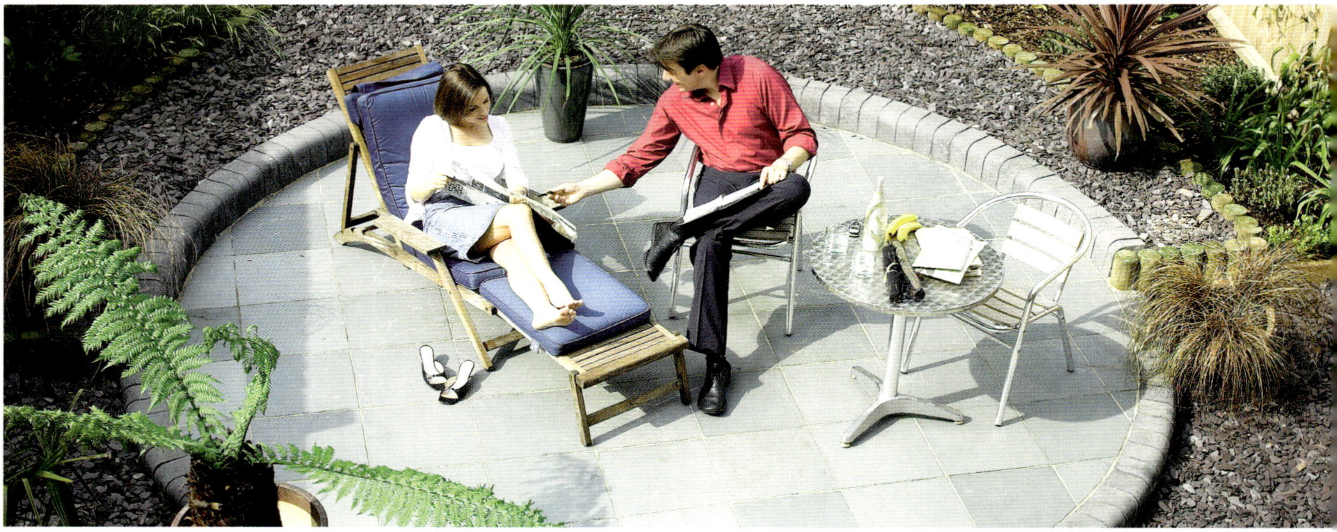

This is a garden for the type of person who, for whatever reason, doesn't have the time or need for a space that requires much maintenance. It is what it is: 'an easy garden'. This garden is ideal for people who winter abroad or who have a second home for the summer. It could be perfect for people who work long hours or are frequent travellers. However, it is basically for anyone who wants a great view and the chance to spend some time in the fresh air, but who has neither the time nor the will to do too much nurturing. I certainly fit into this category. I moved into my house and the garden was a mess. I spent two weeks (my holiday) doing the garden, and in the six months since then I've needed to spend at most an hour or two every other week keeping it in check. It's not that I don't want a garden that requires more attention, but because of what I do I simply don't have time to look after it.

Remember, there is no such thing as a 'no maintenance' garden. This in no way means that the space has to be a totally paved area that has plastic plants and no soul. There are many ways to create a space that, with little effort, can provide all the elements of outdoor living – dining areas, colour all year round, clever use of space, lighting, etc.

Choosing surfaces

The first thing I always say to people when they want an easy garden is 'don't bother with a lawn'. Lawns not only need regular cutting and edging, but also need treatment for weeds and moss. They need feeding, aerating, and raking, all of which takes time you probably don't have. Also, if you are going to be away often your garden

'The first thing I always say to people when they want an easy garden is 'don't bother with a lawn.'

will soon turn into a weed-covered, patchy mess that will ruin the look of your carefully designed garden. In my old garden there was a lawn. During the summer I worked pretty much constantly, and within a month my lawn went from about two inches high and weed-free to a disaster zone crawling with weeds almost waist high. The last thing I felt like doing after a long day at work was getting the mower out; a cold beer and a nice meal were far more appealing options. So think about what you actually use your lawn for. You may put a rug down and sunbathe, and that is probably about it (unless you have kids of course). You can't really put a table and chairs on a lawn for any length of time without them sinking, the barbecue is better placed on a hard surface, and a sunlounger on a patio is far more comfy than a rug on a lawn.

For this type of garden, the hard surfaces will have real implications on the workload involved. Take decking, for example. The great thing about timber decks is the fact that they are

Your garden should include all the elements of outdoor living, so include a decent-sized patio for dining (in the sunniest part of the garden). The usual minimum suitable size is about 3 metres by 3 metres, which is enough for a small table and chairs. Try to install a fitted barbecue because if you travel a lot you won't have to pack it away when you go.

quick, relatively cheap, and easy to install. On the down side, softwood decks have a short life span – anywhere from 10 to 15 years. As with all timber structures in the garden they also need regular treatment with a wood stain or preservative. Decks can also become very slippery when wet, even if they are grooved. Hardwood decks will last longer, but again they need treating and can become slippery. If you are dead set on building a deck, there are some great new alternatives. Try decking that is made from concrete and really does look like the real thing. It is laid just like paving and will last just as long.

The best option for an easy garden is to use paved and brick surfaces, maybe with gravel areas to add texture and colour contrast (see Laying paving and gravel areas, pp.118). All paved areas need is an occasional sweep with a stiff brush and detergent to remove algae, but that's about it, so they are ideal for the easy garden.

Extra features

Make sure you have a small shed for storage; all those gardening tools that you won't be using need somewhere to live. If you have a water feature, make

sure that it is small because ponds need a lot of looking after and fish will need feeding. You will probably want to entertain into the night, so include accent and functional lighting, and even an outdoor heater. You can now buy tabletop heaters that are small enough to store away easily.

Preparing the garden

Preparation is the key, and before you start any kind of work in the garden it is a good idea to remove any trace of weeds. If you have persistent weeds like bindweed you should even sift the soil for their roots; the smallest section left will grow into a new plant.

One of the best time-saving products in gardening is landscape fabric – ideal if you don't have time for weeding. There are quite a few different brands available, and all do pretty much the same thing. All you need to do before you place the plants ready for planting is lay the fabric on all the beds, making sure you overlap any joins so no weeds can sneak through, and pin it in place with staples, which you can buy with the fabric. Then position your plants, cut a cross where you want each one, plant through the fabric, and neatly fold the fabric back around the base of the plants. Finally, lay mulch over the fabric to hide it. There are loads of types of mulch available, from bark chip for a natural effect, to gravel (which is great for a Mediterranean look), to chipped glass, which can look fantastic and is available in many different colours.
I would suggest using chipped bark because it will help your plants remain healthy; it slowly rots down adding essential nutrients to the soil and also helps to retain moisture. A layer of about 3 to 4 inches will do. If you don't use landscape fabric, a thick layer of mulch will still act as a good weed suppressant, but lay it at least 4 to 5 inches deep for best results.

'One of the best time-saving products in gardening is landscape fabric – ideal if you don't have time for weeding. There are quite a few different brands available, and all do pretty much the same thing.'

Irrigation systems

Installing an irrigation system is a must if you want a garden to look after itself. There are many different systems available, from the very simple to ones that are computer-controlled and turn themselves on and off throughout the day. You can have systems installed that will water each plant individually, ones that pop up out of the ground, or even a really simple leaky pipe, which is basically what it sounds like – a pipe with holes all along it. Irrigation systems

are available in most garden centres, and most can be fitted easily. For more complex systems, get a contractor in to do the job.

Making the garden secure

Security will be of utmost importance if you live a busy life and are away a lot. There are a number of physical and psychological deterrents you could include to make the garden safe and secure.

The place to start is with the boundaries; it is essential that they are all sound and in good repair. If you have rear access to your garden, make sure the gate is solid and lockable. Those of you that are techno mad may want to get fingerprint sensors that will only unlock the gate if you are a match. Security lighting that is hooked up to motion sensors will act as a great deterrent to those who venture too close, so install it in all access areas

> 'Natural deterrents are also a very effective means of putting off intruders. Use thorny plants, such as firethorn *(Pyracantha)*, barberry *(Berberis)*, hawthorn, and roses, round the boundaries to act as natural barbed wire. A border that is densely planted will also act as a visual disincentive, offering a tricky route into the garden. So, by planting all the borders to create seclusion, you are adding to your security as well.'

into the garden. If you have a burglar alarm it is possible to extend it to outbuildings, and even to the shed. You can also now get tagging systems, similar to those found in shops, that will set an alarm off if they are taken out of the garden.

Natural deterrents are also a very effective means of putting off intruders. Use thorny plants, such as firethorn *(Pyracantha)*, barberry *(Berberis)*, hawthorn, and roses, round the boundaries to act as natural barbed wire. A border that is densely planted will also act as a visual disincentive, offering a tricky route into the garden. So, by planting all the borders to create seclusion, you are adding to your security as well.

In the home, if you put spiky plants near windows they will put off intruders. The same principle applies in the garden. Gravel paths are noisy to walk on, so make a good security feature on all routes into the garden. Finally, ensure that all tools and valuable items are locked away overnight, and especially if you are going away.

The planting

The main time-consuming element in any garden is obviously the plants, but if you select them carefully you

can limit how much time you will need to spend working in the garden. The best way of creating an easy garden is to choose plants that look after themselves. Avoid anything that needs regular pruning, and also avoid putting many perennials in (which will need deadheading and dividing). So, when you are in the garden centre, ask questions and read labels carefully.

The reason for choosing mostly evergreen shrubs is mainly to provide some kind of interest all year around; you won't end up with empty gaps in the planting during the winter. Plant in groups and then add interest in the front with plants chosen for their striking form, such as Phormiums or yuccas.

Mediterranean-style gravel gardens are great for those of you on a tight schedule, as the gravel mulch will lessen the need for weeding and the plants chosen for this style of garden are used to being neglected. In their natural habitat they have to deal with a lack of water and hot direct sunlight, so they are usually pretty tough.

A top tip for those of you who want low maintenance is to plant lots of ground cover plants. They act much in the same way as a mulch by stopping light getting to the soil surface and controlling weeds.

What I tend to do a couple of evenings per week is to wander around my garden (which doesn't take long – it's tiny!) and remove weeds as soon as I see them. It is best to keep on top of things – little and often is the key – a small weed is easier to remove than one that is entangled around or in a plant. The more you pull out, the less they will keep on coming back.

Planting list

Acer palmatum 'Osakazuki'
Ceratostigma willmottianum
Crinodendron hookerianum
Crocosmia x crocosmiiflora
Dicksonia antarctica
Dicksonia fibrosa
Fatsia japonica
Hosta sieboldiana
Nandina domestica
Panicum virgatum
Pennisetum alopecuroides 'Hamelin'
Phoenix canariensis
Phormium cookianum
Phyllostachys nigra
Phyllostachys aurea
Phyllostachys flexuosa
Phyllostachys aureosulcata var. 'spectabilis'
Phyllostachys aureosulcata var. 'spectabilis'
Polystichum setiferum
Salvia patens
Tricyrtis formosana

As I mentioned earlier, I only spend about an hour every other week in total caring for my garden. I'm lucky to have a sheltered garden in Essex with one of the warmest and driest climates in the country, so I can grow plants that won't survive in cooler parts of the country, such as *Dicksonia*, Phoenix palms, and *Nandina*. However, it proves that you can plant a real mix of interesting plants without having to do loads of work in the garden.

Acer palmatum 'Osakazuki'

Pennisetum alopecuroides 'Hameln'

the traditional garden

The traditional garden is archetypal England: think cream teas, village cricket matches, country pubs, and ploughman's lunches. It might be for those who want to experience a little nostalgia while relaxing, or for someone who wants to preserve a classic style of garden that has withstood the test of time. Grace and elegance are at the heart of this garden; borders are rich, full, and colourful, but neatly contained within their boundaries. Terraces are punctuated with clipped box and topiary, with lavenders for scent; objects like urns, tubs, and statues provide a link with the traditional neo-classical garden style.

Steps and ordered pathways invite you to stroll through arches to secret rose gardens and summer-houses; perfectly smooth lawns surrounded by herbaceous borders offer colour, beauty, and scent. Overall there is a sense of order and restraint. Framed views, focal points, and sheltered walkways draped with vines provide surprises along the way. This is definitely a garden for those who have plenty of time to dedicate to it, and it will suit those who have gardening as a hobby, who can meet the demands of the herbaceous border, keeping the lawn, pruning the roses, shaping and clipping the hedges. Bear in mind that all that digging, raking, and planting is about as good for you as going to the gym, so it's worth it.

'Not many people have the space for a series of grand English garden landscapes, which might include more than one kind of garden, or even a maze.'

This is a garden style steeped in history. In medieval times, sheltered walkways and arbours were essential, enabling ladies to walk in the garden without the risk of loosing their pale complexions (which were thought to be very beautiful). Pergolas were designed to be either free-standing or against buildings and supported roses and vines to create shade. More shade was provided by growing trees around lawns, and benches were placed in sheltered spots to let promenaders sit and eat. In fact, the medievals enjoyed many of the things we associate with a traditional garden today. Turf seats, benches built around trees, seated arbours, trellises, closed board fencing, fish ponds, and even fountains were used from an early date.

Designing a traditional garden

Not many people have the space for a series of grand English garden landscapes, which might include more than one kind of garden, or even a maze. This has led to the development of the mixed border for the small garden where shrubs, perennials, roses, and annuals are all combined together. In the mixed border, larger shrubs provide a solid backdrop. Try to use evergreens, which will remain interesting throughout the seasons. In front, plant a mix of perennials for colour, and foliage plants, or even grasses, for texture. Include bulbs, to pop up every now and then, which can also keep things interesting. Of course, this is all great if you have the space for wide borders. The grand early gardens of the early 19th century had borders that were well over three metres in width. For those of us with small gardens this kind of thing is just not possible. But remember that any kind of border should be at least one metre wide, otherwise you'll have no room for any form of layered planting plan. Plants that work well in the borders will be things such as delphiniums, rudbeckia, hostas, gypsophila, phlox, geranium 'Johnson's Blue', lupins,

When deciding on materials for the garden, it's always good if you can make a visual link back to the house. Say you live in a cottage made from red brick. Try and source bricks to use in the garden that are the same, or as close to the house bricks as possible. The hard landscaping should be discrete. Try and choose materials that are natural in appearance, like natural paving stone, wood, or gravel. This type of garden is a good example of how the space should blend and complement the surroundings. By using local materials, or materials with similar colours, you will create a space that seems in context with the landscape.

Potentilla, Alchemilla mollis – the list goes on. If you have a path it might follow the border edge, so that plants can spill over to soften the hard lines of the landscaping.

Focal points

It is important to have one or more focal points to draw the eye through the space. English gardens were influenced by the Italian and French Renaissance style, which shows in the use of symmetry in design layouts, and with the use of decorative urns, figures, sun dials, and ornate bird baths acting as focal points. I personally love using this kind of thing in traditional gardens.

They are best situated where they will be in full view of a main seating area, or at the far end of a path to entice you to journey through the space. You could accentuate your focal point further by using, for example, a rose arch with a path through it to frame the object. Ornaments will also be effective in other situations as well. Place them either side of a path to set off an entrance. Urns and ornate pots, or even box clipped into balls work well.

If you have a formal area in the garden, such as a walled courtyard, then a centre-piece such as a fountain, pool, or a sun dial will give the space a sense of importance. A carefully placed object peeking out from an herbaceous border or amongst planting can be really effective: a classical statue, or a small pillar set in the midst of ground cover, could create an elysian world of gods and goddesses.

'Try to include a sheltered little hide-away where you can sit and sip drinks in the summer. There are a number of ways of doing this.'

Creating hide-aways

Try to include a sheltered little hide-away where you can sit and sip drinks in the summer. There are a number of ways of doing this. First, you could build a seated arbour (basically a pergola with a bench) and train climbers over it – try a climbing rose and surround it with delicate plants such as forget-me-nots, lavenders, and violets. It is best if this secluded area is not in direct view of the rest of the garden to maintain the sense of privacy. You may remember that in the design section we looked at using circles and squares, which, because of their equal proportions, make good

areas to stop and relax in the garden. If you have a circular area hidden from the main garden surrounded by planting, this makes an ideal place for an old bench, or a spot for a table and chairs.

Secret seating areas create a sense of intrigue throughout the garden. But you can also make a path that curves around a large shrub, so as people turn the corner they are rewarded with another seating area, a pond, a simple view, or an ornament. If visitors to your garden feel a sense of intrigue, then you have done a good job.

Designing a formal area

You could design an area with a fairly formal layout using low, clipped box hedges in simple squares or even more complex patterns. Then plant the

hedged-in area in the manner of a medieval potager, with flowers and vegetables for visual effect. Alternatively, you could plant the clipped box so that it bursts out with lavender or santolina. The best place for an area like this is either by the house, where it will be supported visually by the geometry of the building, or in a walled courtyard or somewhere that has the feel of a self-contained room.

Often you will see formal hedges in traditional gardens cut into turrets, mazes, arches, and all sorts of amazing shapes. Topiary like this takes years of patience, careful clipping, and planning. If you take this challenge on, the best thing to use for a really crisp-looking finish is yew, which has needle-like evergreen foliage and is a really dense plant that can be clipped into very neat shapes, creating fantastic green walls, arches, and a whole host of other possible forms. Holly can be clipped this way, as can cherry laurel *(Osmanthus x burkwoodii)* for a more informal hedge. If you want a shaped hedge it is a good idea to continue the theme through the rest of the garden to create a visual link, much in the way you would with other materials. For example, if you have clipped box spheres as an entrance to a formal lawn,

'Secret seating areas create a sense of intrigue throughout the garden. But you can also make a path that curves around a large shrub, so as people turn the corner they are rewarded with another seating area, a pond, a simple view, or an ornament.'

and a back-drop of neatly shaped yew, this will create a strong formal style and a sense of continuity to the design.

Mixing formal and informal elements

The decision on whether your garden is going to be formal, informal, or both is totally up to you, a matter of personal taste and how much time you have to spend. Keeping hedges and a formal garden in trim is going to take work and time for it to become established, and is a real labour of love. An informal

traditional garden to me is what I dream of, when I have the time and space to do it. The connection with nature and its surroundings makes the space sit effortlessly, with sweeping curves, pergolas, hidden seating areas, covered walkways, and a relaxed feel to rival any other garden style. Mixing elements of the formal with the informal, such as neo-classical focal points, topiary, or even a Romanesque structure can have a striking effect, bringing order and punctuation to the garden. The traditional English garden has developed over the years with an amalgamation of different styles and features that have stood the test of time extremely well. A walk through a garden should be a journey with surprises around every corner. The blend of the formal with the informal never fails to excite. From crisp, clipped hedges to vivid borders, and secret nooks to babbling brooks, there is something peaceful and timeless about the English garden.

Planting list

Alchemilla mollis
Anemnonme x hybrida
Buxus sempeivirens
Delphiniums
Euphorbia griffithii
Geranium 'Johnson's Blue'
Gypsophila
Honeysuckle
Hostas
Laburnum
Lavenders
Lupins
Osmanthus
Phlox
Potentilla
Roses
Rudbeckia
Santolina
Stachys lanata
Viburnum
Vines
Wisteria

Elements

- Arbours
- Arches
- Bird baths
- Brick and stone walling
- Brick pathways
- Classical statues
- Gazebos
- Herb gardens
- Herbaceous borders
- Lawns (trimmed like bowling greens!)
- Natural sandstone paving
- Pergola
- Ponds
- Symmetry
- Topiary
- Urns

Roses

Phlox

the rustic garden

The rustic garden aims to capture the charm and simplicity of life in rural France, Spain, or Italy. It's for people who fell in love with Provence or Tuscany on their first visit and now want to recreate the feeling they had there at home. Let's face it, the British garden doesn't exactly offer us endless days of sunshine and warmth, but that doesn't mean we can't have a garden with a Mediterranean look and feel – one that reminds us of the laid-back attitude of the Mediterranean culture. This garden is all about the dream of living life like the southern Europeans do; where everything is more relaxing and enjoying life is more important than work or money.

Getting the rustic look

Rustic gardens need not be expensive to create. For example, the garden furniture can have a basic wooden construction, and a 'weathered' or 'distressed' look is ideal since it reflects the outdoor lifestyle and will blend in with the natural surroundings. Choose weathered tones of bleached wood and stone, and then contrast them with the warm colour of terracotta. The garden should have a sleepy atmosphere, almost as if it has been mellowed over the years by the heat. The planting should be striking and fragrant. The various elements of the garden need to be placed carefully to effectively contrast areas of light and shade. Bear this in mind if you create vine-covered pergolas, which evoke life under the sun so well.

This garden will appeal to those of you who are searching for an air of tranquillity, and who want a space to breathe easy in – an oasis of calm. It won't be low maintenance; you'll need

'This garden will appeal to those of you who are searching for an air of tranquillity and want a space where you can breathe easy.'

to spend a bit of time looking after it. On the other hand, it certainly isn't for those of you who think that everything should have its place or who need to be surrounded by order. This garden is an organic thing that needs the freedom to grow and develop its own character over the years.

The rustic garden conjures up images of a rural lifestyle when anything modern seems out of place, a garden where only you and the surrounding countryside exist. Nothing useful is thrown away and the garden is full of old artefacts left behind by the generations of people who have lived there before you. Sounds idyllic. However, designing this type of garden can be a challenge because it is a space that needs to develop over the years, and it can look contrived if done badly. So here are a few ways to get the look you're after.

You should avoid any kind of formality in the space; rely on informal shapes to create a relaxed and natural feeling. The garden won't have a rigid design

that needs to be maintained; it will change and mature, and that is exactly the point of this garden. It is ideal for the type of person who likes to do things slowly.

Getting in a contractor to build your garden and create a perfectly formed space all in one go won't really work for

Your choice of hard materials will have a big influence on how authentic your rustic look is. Terracotta tiles are one of the most obvious things to use; their warm colour is fundamental to the look. Many different types are available, ranging from original terracotta to concrete reproductions, and they come in various shapes and sizes. Choose from squares, rectangles, or some of the other shapes ideally suited to create complex designs and patterns. Riven pavers have a rustic look and will create a seating area with an aged feel.

the rustic garden. Your garden will be far more pleasing and authentic-looking if you let it develop over a few years, so don't rush it! You still can install the bare bones of the design – such as the patio, paths, pergolas, pots, and all the various elements – but be flexible, moving things around now and again and adding items that you collect over the years.

Preparing a garden to entertain in

Entertaining is at the heart of this garden. Barbecues for family and friends are a regular event, so a large patio area with a fitted barbecue, chimenea, or clay oven is needed, as well as plenty of space for chairs, tables, and benches. This space should have a cosy feel so avoid a wide open patio. Try to create

a sense of intimacy and being enclosed: decorate the area with loads of terracotta pots and planters, full of colourful flowers such as geraniums and violas. Plant all around the area with fragrant plants such as lavenders, santolina, and herbs that can be used in cooking and on the barbie. Try to entice the garden onto the walls of the house: grow climbers on trellis, or use a pergola or wall shrubs. Aim to have lots of pots with colourful and trailing plants hanging on the walls. Doing this will help create a seamless transition between house and garden.

Loads of companies now sell rustic garden furniture on the Internet, in shops, and in garden centres. Choose things that look as though you've made them yourself, or if you are a bit handy, do so. With its basic design and round timbers that look sun-bleached, this kind of furniture has real rural charm. I wouldn't go over the top though. If all your furniture is like this, it may look contrived, so have a few benches too. Maybe put one on the patio and another at the other end of the garden in a secret seating area, flanked by a couple of terracotta pots full of bright red geraniums.

'There are now loads of companies selling rustic garden furniture on the Internet, in shops, and in garden centres, so choose things that look although you have made them yourself, or if you are a bit handy, do so. Usually made from round timbers that look sun bleached, and basic in design, this kind of furniture has real rural charm.'

You will need a sheltered area on or near the patio, and the most authentic way of achieving this is with a pergola. I was staying in Cyprus with a Greek family a few years ago and their kitchen (which always smelt of home cooking) led straight out onto a patio with a huge pergola overhead. Growing all over it was a thirty-year-old vine with grapes hanging down all over the place, and growing through it was a white jasmine that smelt fantastic and sweet. For me, this is how the rustic garden should be and you can easily create this look in your garden. Grape 'brant' *(Vitis brant)* is a vigorous vine that within a few years will easily cover a medium-sized pergola. When the sun shines through, it creates a beautiful dappled shade in which to escape the hot summer sun. You can make the pergola

from standard treated timber or use equestrian poles (round poles), which will give an even more rustic feel.

Creating rustic charm

To make the garden look as if it has been there for years, you will need to have a collection of old bits and bobs that say 'rustic charm'. Old tools are a must – simply place them amongst plants, leaning them up against an old rickety fence. Use milk urns, mill stones – whatever you can think of that will add charm to the space. There are loads of places to find such objects and I bet it'll become a bit of an obsession. Look in reclamation yards, antique shops, and skips (ask permission first). Go to boot sales and house sales. You can even find suitable items on walks along the beach or in the countryside (but be aware that it's illegal to remove some items from such places). Look for old oil drums that can be planted, chimney pots, even old suitcases – anything that can be used as a quirky feature in the garden. There are no rules so have fun with it and try things in different positions in the garden.

The planting

The planting in this garden will have some Mediterranean influence. The plants will be chosen to provide aroma,

flowers, and fruit. Olive trees are becoming widely available these days and in warmer areas of the country they will survive outdoors during winter. I have one in a pot that I keep indoors in the winter and move onto the patio during the summer. I'm sure it would be fine outside but, quite simply, it makes a great house plant too. Olive trees have tiny white flowers during the summer that are actually quite fragrant and are followed by the fruit (olives) in autumn. Olive trees are quite slow-growing and can live for hundreds of years. I love these trees because they become all twisted, knotted, and full of character. They're perfect for the rustic garden.

'To make the garden look as if it has been there for years you will need to have a collection of old bits and bobs, so that it has that feeling of rustic charm. Old tools are a must, simply place them amongst plants lean them against an old rickety fence. Use milk urns, mill stones, whatever you can think of that will add charm to the space.'

Citrus plants

Citrus fruits are a must for this garden but they won't be happy outside during the winter; keep them in pots so you can bring them inside. Citrus trees and shrubs have highly fragrant, mostly white flowers. They are evergreen and will need to be in a sunny spot. They don't like being moved too often, so bring them out for the summer and leave them where they are until you bring them in again for the winter. Once inside, they will need to be in a warm conservatory or by a sunny window. Mist and water them often.

Loquat

Another interesting fruit tree is the loquat *(Eriobotrya japonica),* which likes a sheltered, sunny spot. This semi-evergreen tree grows quite happily in sheltered gardens and tolerates temperatures as low as -5°C, but not for very long periods. In autumn, it bears fragrant, white flowers followed by small orange-yellow fruits that are edible. In places like Portugal, they are used to make preserves and chutneys.

Herbs and aromatic plants

Herbs and aromatic plants are a must. The first plant that is essential to have is the bay laurel *(Laurus nobilis)*. This tree or shrub grows to around 10 metres in height if left to do its own thing. Has clusters of green-yellow flowers in spring, and on female plants they look like little black berries after flowering. Even though they grow very large, bays do tolerate clipping well. You can buy them as standard small trees (like lollipops) with twining stems, which look great in pots on any patio. They like to have shelter from cold, drying winds so put them

in a warm sheltered spot in sun or part-shade. Other herbs and plants to try, include chives, dill, fennel, borage, mint, basil, parsley, thyme, rosemary, sage, onions, garlic, artichokes, etc.

Lavender
Lavender is a fantastic aromatic plant, found in dry areas throughout the Mediterranean. There are lots of different ones around but all of them like full sun and well-drained soil (which makes sense if you look at where they are from). My favourite is French lavender *(Lavandula stoechas)*, which is the most elegant. Each flower spike has wings that look like little purple rabbit ears on its tip. Lavender has lots of nectar so bees love it. It works well in pots, along paths, as a low hedge, or in the border. Most varieties range from frost hardy to fully hardy and make a colourful, aromatic addition to any garden.

The rustic look and feel

- Old 'junk', carefully chosen and positioned
- Old-looking materials
- Grape vines
- Gravel, brick, or tile paths
- Herbs
- Laid-back feel
- Light and shade
- Mediterranean planting (silver foliage)
- Mediterranean life – good social life, wine, 'outdoor life', family, cosy, care-free, laid-back
- Natural materials
- Olive trees
- Patios
- Pergola
- Scents – floral, citrus, herbal
- Simple wooden furniture
- Soft lines
- Speckled sunlight shining through vine leaves
- Terracotta pavers and tiles
- Terracotta pots and wall hangings
- Trellis
- Warm vivid colours

Planting list

Aloe vera
Chives
Citrus trees
Cypress
Echinops
Fennel
Ficus carica
Geranium
Jasmine
Laurus nobilis
Lavenders
Limonium
Loquat
Myrtle
Oleander
Olive trees
Perovskia 'Blue spire'
Rosemary
Santolina
Vitis brant

Citrus trees

Lavender

the exotic garden

The exotic garden is for those with a sense of adventure. As people travel more than ever before and experience exotic places, they want to be able to capture the feeling they had on holiday and somehow preserve it in their home and garden. It can be a challenge, but that is half the fun. There is something really special about arriving in a garden with banana trees, tree ferns, bamboos, and all sorts of red-hot colours. This garden can be any size and is possible to achieve in our climate: not all exotic plants are 'tender', and there are plenty of other reliable plants that give the impression of being exotic but grow well here.

The exotic garden is an enduring source of wonder for the person who creates it and for those who visit. It allows endless opportunities for storytelling – you can talk about where the plants come from, who discovered them, and how they are nurtured through the eccentricities of the British climate. Such a garden might capture the sun-soaked vibrancy of Latin America, Mexico, or North Africa, or the wild beauty of New Zealand. Tropical, desert, structural, bold: whatever you go for, the style of this garden will be determined by who you are and what you are like. If you wish, it can even be an exciting collage of styles and influences.

What is exotic?

If you look up the meaning of the word 'exotic', you will come across words such as unusual, striking, bizarre, mysterious, colourful, foreign, glamorous, and, best of all, outlandish. Put in these terms, an exotic garden suddenly starts to look even more appealing. An exotic garden fits into two categories: the lush jungle garden

'What you actually choose to put in this garden will very much depend on what your take is on the word 'exotic'.'

or the dry Mediterranean garden. In both, the exotic look is created primarily by the plants, but your choice of hard materials also plays a large part.

What you actually choose to put in this garden will very much depend on what your take is on the word 'exotic'. When I started thinking about how I would design this type of garden, I realised that most, if not all, gardens have at least a few elements of the exotic. Loads of plants that are now commonplace in the UK originate in far-flung corners of the globe. Take magnolias, for example. If you drive anywhere in London in spring, you will see hundreds of magnolias with their opulent blooms in pink, white, and creamy yellow growing happily all over the place. In fact, they come from places like the USA, Nepal, China, Japan, India, Tibet, Burma, Bhutan, and the list goes on. If that's not exotic, what is?! The same applies to some of the most commonly used garden plants: from lupins to lilies and hydrangeas to hyacinths. But these plants are now so common that they don't seem 'exotic' any more, so the search for the still more unusual continues.

Unfortunately, not many of us get the chance to travel the world looking for new and unusual plants to grow in our small patch in suburbia. However, it's possible to create a feeling of the exotic with relative ease, or take it one step further and create a plant collector's garden full of tender plants and exotica that all need careful nurturing.

The 'lush jungle'

I believe most people's idea of an exotic garden falls into the 'lush jungle' style. This garden conjures up images of tropical or sub-tropical forests. It is calming, peaceful, and a million miles away from the office and all the stresses and strains of life. This type of garden will need plenty of moisture and shade. Planting will include all the different shades of green, with large-leaved plants providing a dramatic contrast to the spiky ones.

Bamboos work fantastically well in this type of garden and are widely available. The larger ones such as Timber bamboo *(Phyllostachys bambusoides)*, Golden bamboo *(P. aurea)*, and Black bamboo *(P. nigra)* are all great for creating instant screens and achieving height in the garden. I have four different types of *Phyllostachys* in my garden, and as soon as I planted them my garden instantly felt more established, with added height and movement.

Plants with a strong, spiky form are essential and very eye-catching, especially when planted amongst softer, large-leaved plants. Try things like phormiums and cordylines. Phormiums come in quite a few varieties, ranging from the massive *Phormium tenax* to the smaller *P.* 'Bronze baby', which is a dwarf hybrid of the former. They have long, pointed, strap-like leaves that turn into a V-shape at the base and come in a range of colours. The cultivars have a great range with variegated leaves as well. Phormiums also produce tall summer spikes of tubular flowers that shoot out from the middle of the clump, up to about 12 feet high on the bigger varieties. *P. tenax* is only suitable for a large space because each leaf can grow to about 3 metres (10 feet) in length. In a small garden, it's best to try the slightly smaller *P. cookianum*, *P.* 'Bronze baby', *P.* 'Yellow wave', or one of the other smaller cultivars. Be aware that the more colourful ones seem to be less hardy, so plant them in a sheltered spot.

To create a 'lush' feeling, the most reliable things to go for are plants such as the Japanese aralia *(Fatsia japonica)*, which comes from coastal woodland in Japan and South Korea. It's a really valuable plant because it's as tough as old boots and can tolerate pollution as well as a coastal position. It has huge, hand-shaped, thick, leathery green leaves. It can get as high as 2 metres tall and grows even wider than that.

In autumn, it has creamy-white flowers like little balls on the end of groups of long spikes. All in all, it's a great plant for achieving that lush, tropical look.

'There are many tropical plants that can be grown in the garden during the summer, but these will need winter protection. While this sounds daunting, in reality, with some plants it is pretty simple.

Winter protection

There are many tropical plants that can be grown in the garden during the summer, but these will need winter protection. While this sounds daunting, in reality, with some plants it is pretty simple.

Ginger lilies

Ginger lilies are fantastic and the most readily available is *Cautleya spicata*, which is a rhizomatous perennial from the Himalayas. It has lush, mid-green leaves and spikes and yellow flowers with maroon bracts. It grows up to 90 cm tall and is fairly hardy. It should be grown in a semi-shady border with humus-rich soil and plenty of moisture. Most importantly, over the winter apply a really thick mulch to protect the rhizome from hard frosts. Another lily to recommend is *Hedychium*, which is also a rhizomatous perennial and the best known of the ginger lilies. When it comes to being frost tender, it is borderline but more reliable than many others. It is valued for its tropical lance-shaped leaves, as well as its very tall flower spikes which reach heights of 2–3 metres. Other ginger lilies to try are *H. forrestii*, and *H. densiflorum*. I know a chap in Norwich who grows, amongst others, *H. greenei* with great success. All may survive a mild frost over the winter but only if given a thick protective mulch to help them through.

Indian shot plant

Indian shot plant *(Canna)* is another well-known plant that is ideal for a lush garden. Personally, I love the lush foliage but the flowers are a little too much for me. They are frost tender but thankfully they are easy to propagate and look after. In early spring, you will find them easily at the garden centre as tubers and later on as potted and ready for planting. If you want to keep them going year after year, once the leaves are turned black by the frost dig them up and cut off the dead foliage to about 5 cm from the ground. Store in a frost-free place (a well-ventilated box with dry bark chips works well), and continue to check them throughout the winter, chucking away any rotting ones. Then next year, when you want to prepare them for planting, put each tuber in a 15 cm pot (with the growing tip pointing up of course!) and cover with normal potting compost, leaving the tip just popping out of the surface. They need to be kept moist at about 20°C until they are about 18–20 cm tall and then you can stick them somewhere cooler like a window sill until the risk of frost has gone and you can plant them out. It is really good fun reusing plants like this and is well worth the small amount of effort involved. The tropical-looking foliage is invaluable in an exotic garden.

Palms

No exotic garden would be complete without using some kind of palm or palm-like plant. An invaluable plant due to its exotic palm-like foliage has to be the banana; the most widely available is Japanese banana *(Musa basjoo),* which is also among the hardiest. It is actually an evergreen, suckering perennial that makes a great specimen plant. The only trouble is they don't like strong winds, which shred the leaves, and they also don't like frost. Smaller ones can be kept in pots and moved inside during winter or, if planted, protected with an old chimney pot or large drain-pipe stuffed with straw. The chap in Norwich I mentioned earlier has got a *Musa basjoo* in his tropical garden that has been outside for ten years. What he does is cut it down to the upright stem when the frost has blackened the leaves. Then he builds a tower around the stems with pallets and back-fills with straw, finally topped off with a bit of roofing felt to protect it from rain. I know this sounds like a bit of a mission but it probably only takes a couple of hours and in my mind is well worth it.

In your exotic garden, palms will add a sense of structure and act as focal points. A few are guaranteed to survive in our climate, the most reliable of which is the Chusan palm *(Trachycarpus fortunei)*. It will survive temperatures as low as –15°C. It is usually single-stemmed with huge, fan-shaped mid-green leaves that can become massive – up to 1 metre across.
It can grow up to about 6–7 metres tall and enjoys sun or part-shade, but will not like strong or cold winds. There are smaller varieties such as the miniature Chusan palm *(T. wagnerianus)*, or the Yunnan dwarf palm *(T. nanus),* which is almost trunkless and an endangered species in the wild. If you can find a cultivated one, it will make a real talking point. Jelly palm *(Butia capitata)* is often available at specialist palm centres and I have to admit that opinions are divided regarding its suitability to the English garden. Some books say that it will not withstand long periods below 0°C, and

others say that mature specimens can withstand –10°C. If you get a small one, I would suggest you bring it inside during the winter, and once it gets bigger, leave it out but protect it during winter with fleece. It may be a bit of a risk but that's part of the fun of having an exotic garden – trying things out to see if you can get them to survive. A great palm for a smaller garden is the Dwarf fan palm *(Chamaerops humilis)*, which has fan-like leaves. It varies greatly in size, with some growing only a few feet and others getting up to 6–7 feet tall. In terms of hardiness, it is second only to the Chusan palm *(Trachycarpus fortunei)*, but it may need some winter protection.

A very popular palm, which you see everywhere, is the Cabbage palm *(Cordyline australis)*. This plant is almost a standard feature in gardens these days. When young, it is like a little fountain of sword-like leaves which shoot up from the base, eventually forming a tall thin trunk of up to 10 metres. Most varieties will survive the frost, but it won't hurt to tie up the leaves and wrap them during cold winters.

'By far, ferns are my favourite element in an exotic garden, especially tree ferns. These are one of the most ancient types of plant with fossilized remains dating back millions of years. It's a bit of a mad thought that dinosaurs may well have been munching the same type of plant that we are using in our gardens.

Tree ferns

By far, ferns are my favourite element in an exotic garden, especially tree ferns. These are one of the most ancient types of plant with fossilized remains dating back millions of years. It's a bit of a mad thought that dinosaurs may well have been munching the same type of plant that we are using in our gardens. Tree ferns have an incredibly prehistoric look. The trunks grow slowly, only about 4–5 cm a year, so take that into account when you buy them (the larger ones reflect this in their price). On the plus side, even on one that is 40 cm tall you could end up with some amazing fronds as large as a metre long. Tree ferns are truly the most magnificent of all the ferns, but you must care for them correctly. The trunk is actually part of the root system of the plant, which is exposed to the air, so this must be kept moist at all times. Be especially vigilant if you live in a very dry area; a drip irrigation system directed into the crown (where the fronds come from) is a good option. The most common variety is the soft tree fern *(Dicksonia antarctica)*. They are classed as frost hardy to frost tender, which basically means frost could be a problem for them. But, saying that, I have one in a shady, sheltered corner that has dealt with snow and frost perfectly well. In their natural habitat, it can get as cold as –10°C, so they should be OK. As they are quite expensive, I took a bit of a risk doing this. If you don't want to risk it, protect the crown over the winter by bending some of the fronds inwards to the crown and stuffing the crown with straw or covering it with horticultural fleece.

The tree fern works well with other low-level ferns such as buckler fern *(Dryopteris)*, shield fern *(Polystichum)*, or the more unusual *Polypodium*, some of which are hardy and others tender. Other tree ferns you could try include the golden tree fern *(Dicksonia fibrosa)*, the very unusual New Zealand tree fern *(Dicksonia squarrosa)*, or the Wheki tree fern, which has a tall, thin trunk. Unlike any other tree fern, it can branch out and may form a spreading clump.

The exotic city garden

Cities are a good few degrees warmer than the surrounding countryside, so the choice of suitable exotic plants will be far greater for city dwellers. The trick is to achieve a real mixture of textures and shades, combining green, paddle-leaved plants like bananas with bamboos, lush ferns, grasses, palms, and perennials. The result will be a calming, sheltered microclimate in which you can escape reality. After all, an exotic garden is an opportunity for your imagination to run riot.

What I would try to achieve with the overall design of a city garden would be a central seating area surrounded by 'walls' of lush foliage. The feeling you would want to create would be one of seclusion – try imagining yourself in a Jurassic jungle and that's what the garden should feel like. The whole garden doesn't need to be created like that, just an area of it. The materials you use should all have a natural look such as slate, terracotta, stone, and wood. Hardwood decking in particular will contrast beautifully with the lush planting. You may want to include a water feature of some kind; I would suggest a still pool to make the garden seem like some secret romantic place. Adventure is the key, so try and use some ancient-looking artefacts, or maybe pieces you have collected on your travels. Carefully place them amongst the plants to create an impression of being lost in a place that time forgot. This garden is a real talking point so don't hold back – the more curiosities and opportunities for stories you can introduce the better.

The Mediterranean look

Another idea for the exotic garden is to try and achieve a Mediterranean look. Try placing exotic plants in a Moorish setting. Imagine the vibrant colours of Morocco and southern Spain: the fabulous blue and white tiles; the terracottas and warm shades of orange and red. Create paved areas that have a mosaic in the centre of them using tiles reminiscent of those found in a Moorish courtyard. Use arches inspired by the ancient architecture and echo this shape in trellising and mirrors and on walls: cut 'windows' in trellis panels, cut shapes out of sheets of exterior ply, or paint the arch shape on to walls. Create curving or formal raised beds and paint them a vivid colour or cover them with small tiles. Attach a chunky timber coping to act as a bench.

The beauty of this type of garden is that there aren't many design restrictions. It is an opportunity for you to get really creative with shapes, colours, materials, and plants. Without meaning to sound like a broken record, always bear in mind the basic design rules regarding informal and formal gardens. The jungle feel will be far more effective in an informal setting because you are trying to recreate a natural feel. The Mediterranean style could be either informal or formal, but it will suit a formal layout especially well.

Planting list

Plants for architecture
Brahea armarta
Chamaerops humilis
Cordyline australis
Dicksonia antarctica
Dicksonia fibrosa
Dicksonia squarrosa
Phoenix canariensis
Phormium
Trachycarpus fortunei
Trachycarpus nanus
Trachycarpus wagnerianus

Bamboos
Chusquea gigantean
Fargesia
Phyllostachys
Pleioblastus
Sasa

Plants for fruit and flowers
Abutilon
Arbutus unedo
Brugmansia aurea
Cautleya
Crocosmia x crocosmiiflora
Curcuma
Hedychium spicatum
Luma apiculata

Plants for lush foliage
Alocasia
Aucuba japonica
Cannas
Colocasia
Ensete ventricosum
Fastia japonica
Gunnera manicata
Hosta sieboldiana
Mahonia japonica
Musa basjoo
Pittosporum tobira
Rheum

Brugmansia datura

Musa basjoo

the designer garden

This is a garden for the sophisticated minimalist. The owners of this garden are probably really busy, successful professionals, and their homes will be simple yet smartly functional, with sleek Scandinavian lines (a bit like me). These people will want a garden that looks good all year around but has a sense of control and calm. Nothing is random, and over time the garden will evolve – but not chaotically. The design will contain everything in its rightful place, with clean, sharp lines barely softened by planting. Carefully chosen sculpture and hard landscaping will play a major role, with architectural plants adding a strong sense of form and structure to the space. In a way this style of garden is a living work of modern art, far more a Mondrian than a Monet.

A well-designed garden

Designer as a word means chic, fashionable, stylish, expensive, and exclusive, which to me sounds a bit out of reach and unobtainable. That really isn't the case. A designer garden is actually within the reach of those with a small budget, as well as those with a large budget. A designer look can be achieved with cheaper materials such as decking and gravel, or you can really push the boat out with expensive natural stones and sculptures. However, at the end of the day, it doesn't matter how much you have to spend on a garden. A well 'designed' garden is a well-designed garden.

Minimalism and modernism

Minimalism is more of a design movement than a 'designer style'. Take fashion for example – there are lots of different styles from different designers.

'Designer as a word means chic, fashionable, stylish, expensive, and exclusive, which to me sounds a bit out of reach and unobtainable. That really isn't the case.'

Minimalism is just part of many other styles in a contemporary designed garden. Minimalism goes hand in hand with modernism as a reaction against very stylistic movements such as Art Nouveau. Minimalism was a style that searched for pureness of form through truth and simplicity, and it was the basis for the argument that 'form follows function'. I'd say a designer garden is one that reflects a contemporary style that could include modernism, minimalism, purism, and even eclectic styles. So, if you take the word contemporary and what it means, you may come up with words such as modern, current, fashionable, and of course 'designer', and at the moment minimalism and simplicity is the kind of style that the owner of a designer garden will be looking for.

Using the house

The best place to start designing this type of garden is to look back at the house and pick some of the dominant features. Use these to create a grid (see Design Basics,). It is far easier to create a modern minimalist garden for a modern house, but that is not to say you cannot have this type of garden on an older style property. Just make sure to use the dominant lines of the house as a basis for the design and maybe make some kind of historical reference back to the architecture within the design.

I would almost always choose straight lines as the basis for the minimalist

Minimalism is perfectly suited to garden design because less is often more in terms of gardens. This approach leads to an uncluttered space that can be easy to maintain and creates a cool, calming atmosphere. I think atmosphere is an important word in this case because this will not be a garden for everybody. Some may consider it cold, stark, and lifeless, whereas to others it will feel clean, controlled, and sleek. It will differ greatly in atmosphere to, say, the exotic or the rustic garden, which will feel as if they have always been there. A designer garden will look 'designed', and that's the whole point!

look and use these to link the house and garden. I'm not saying you cannot use curves and circles, but I would keep them away from the house – maybe as a seating area or lawn. Large glass doors leading into the garden are always a great feature, and a continuous link between the indoors and garden works well with the minimalist look. I have a wooden floor in my living room and am lucky enough to have French doors to the garden, so what I did is build a timber deck outside at the same height as the living room to form a seamless link. So, by using similar materials inside and out, there is unity between the interior and the garden, and by using a dominant feature (the French doors) there is unity between the architecture and the garden.

Spaces and focal points

A formal minimal style is best suited for this type of garden because order and a sense of control are vital in the design process and in the finished garden. Spaces need to be clearly defined. Uncluttered, open spaces with simple planting are the key. Avoid any kind of redundant decoration. This will lead to a calm, collected, modern space, uninterrupted from clutter, that will have beauty through simplicity.

In a garden such as this you will want to choose a focal point that really makes a statement. Because the garden itself is uncluttered, a centrepiece that has visual impact will help add interest to the space. You could use a water feature with water cascading over a wall like sheet glass, a sculpture, or even a bespoke outdoor room to house a jacuzzi, office, or sanctuary space.

'In a garden such as this you will want to choose a focal point that really makes a statement. Because the garden itself is uncluttered, a centrepiece that has visual impact will help add interest to the space.'

Choosing materials

The materials you choose should be clean and crisp in appearance. Old Yorkstone, tatty old sleepers, anything 'oldie worlde' will look right out of place, so look at things like slate, granite paving, hardwood decking, stainless steel, glass, and all the kinds of materials you would expect to see in 'designer homes'. Keep the colour palette in the materials pure and simple, and choose one main element, such as pressed granite paving, and use it throughout the whole garden to give a sense of continuity to the space.

Under foot you should choose materials that are free of any pattern, such as concrete pavers, pale smooth limestone, or marble, all of which should be laid to perfection: leave smaller joints than you usually would and select slabs that are as large as possible. By choosing light-coloured materials you will be reflecting not only the light but also the pureness of the design. Polished concrete is a fantastic cheap alternative to expensive stones. It can be dyed and formed to any shaped area, giving a slightly more refined look. Resin-bonded gravel is another great surface, giving you the option to choose any type of aggregate that you like.

Surfaces like decking should be constructed using hardwoods such as red cedar, balau, ipe, or tatajuba, which have a more refined look than softwoods and will last much longer. They look better if you can get them un-grooved (yes, I know, it's more slippery when wet, but this garden is about a refined simple look). Steel grid panels and tread plate surfaces can also work well but will cost quite a lot to install. Red wood decks set out in a grid pattern with thin, stainless steel frames look amazing, or even try decking and steel grid panels as a striking minimalist surface. Cobbles, setts, and smaller paving units can also be used in the space, creating a textured surface that can be treated as a uniformed whole rather than bitty individual elements. Also, don't forget grass. Again, this will need to be laid absolutely perfectly and be beautifully maintained, but it makes a really good soft surface that will contrast well with the other materials. The most important thing is to not have too many materials going on, as this will just lead to a confused, and certainly not minimal, space.

Solid boundaries are important in the garden, and if you can use the same material as the floors you will achieve a real sense of continuity. Breezeblocks and rendered walls painted a suitable colour are quite a cheap option, and glass or timber screens look fantastic. In this style of garden you will often

see raised beds and walls made from breezeblocks that are rendered and painted white or cream. This works really well because you can create varying levels within the space and they act as a fantastic backdrop to planting.

> 'In this style of garden you will often see raised beds and walls made from breezeblocks that are rendered and painted white or cream. This works really well because you can create varying levels within the space and they act as a fantastic backdrop to planting.'

Light and colour

Because the actual design of the garden is simple and pure, light and colour will play a major role in creating the atmosphere of the space. Dynamic effects can be created with clever manipulation of light and colour. Take walls, for example. A breezeblock wall painted white is quite bland and uninteresting on its own. But if you cut two square holes in it, first the wall becomes more dynamic, and, second, light will seep through the holes adding further atmosphere to the space. You could even position plants in the line of light. Glass panels acting as screens with some areas frosted and others not, curved steel walls, coloured perspex, or glass panels – all of these will create interesting light effects. Try also installing lighting to create mood, accentuate planting, and illuminate utility areas.

Colours should be clean and neutral, but not necessarily monochromatic. There is room for more vivid colour schemes, such as black and white, but they have to be carefully considered.

Adding water features

Water features can add a soothing element to a refined and simple space. There is no doubt that the sound of running water is a soothing experience, and the reflective qualities of water can be useful in a design. A reflective pool will add a sense of stillness to the space and will reflect plants and even the sky, adding a new dimension to the garden. On the other hand, flowing water, like water on glass sheets, adds a sophisticated air.

Water features in this garden will tend to be expensive, often also doubling as works of art, but there are cheaper items around. Try drilled slate monoliths or metallic spheres. You could have a rill running through the garden, a deck that appears to float on a still pool (in actual fact all you need is a thin channel around the edges), raised pools with coping that acts as seats, water jets leaping around the space, or even subtle fountains, but remember that this is a space for peace and quiet, so don't let them get too noisy.

The planting

The plants will have a controlled appearance to them – this is not a garden for invasive plants that are going to escape their confines and make the garden look wild. Architectural plants, bamboos, grasses, neatly trimmed box, lavender hedges, and Japanese maples are far more the look you'll be after.

I find that planting big groups of one plant together often has more impact that mixing stuff. This garden is all about structure and creating a sense of order, so show this in the way it is planted. For example, tall screens of bamboo are a great way to create divides and screens – they can be used on all sides of a seating area, creating living walls. Grasses work particularly well planted en-masse, making a bold textural statement.

I would also suggest that this be more of a garden for foliage than flowers. By all means use some flowering plants, but keep them and their colours to a minimum. Control being the key,

choose one, two, or at the most three flower colours as your theme in the planting. Try blue, white, or purple, and choose colours that complement each other.

It is worth spending a bit extra on mature plants that will give you that instant look, and by introducing plants such as clipped box you will add a sense of permanence and punctuation, through simple and pure forms. The one saving grace in this garden is that planting can be kept to a minimum. It often works well just to choose two or three main plants to repeat throughout the space, such as bamboo *(Phyllostachys nigra)*, a grass *(Carex buchananii)*, and an evergreen, the cherry laurel *(Prunus laurocerasus* 'Otto luyken').

As a contrast to the simplicity of the design you may want to introduce one or two plants with a 'wow' factor. Spiky plants such as phormiums, yuccas, and cordylines will add contrast to softer grasses and billowing bamboos, or a New Zealand tree fern *(Dicksonia squarrosa)* could add an element of height to the garden. These plants will grab your attention and add architectural interest, working well with the hard landscaping, and they can even be used as focal points in the place of garden ornaments and sculptures.

In summary

This garden will require planning and careful consideration. There may be some elements that will need specialised contractors for advice and installation. Just remember that less is more, and that you are working with not only hard landscaping and plants, but with light, colour, atmosphere, reflection, etc., all of which will bring a dynamic feel to a pure and simple space.

Planting list

Acer davidii
Acer griseum
Betula pendula laciniata
Buxus sempevirens
Buxus microphylla
Carex buchananii
Cordyline australis
Dicksonia antarctica
Dicksonia fibrosa
Dicksonia squarrosa
Lavandula angustifolia
Nandina domestica
Ophiopogon planiscapus nigrescens
Pennisetum
Phormium
Phyllostachys
Stipa tenuifolia
Trachycarpus fortunei
Verbena bonariensis
Yucca filamentos
Yucca gloriosa

Phyllostachys

Dicksonia antarctica

the psi garden

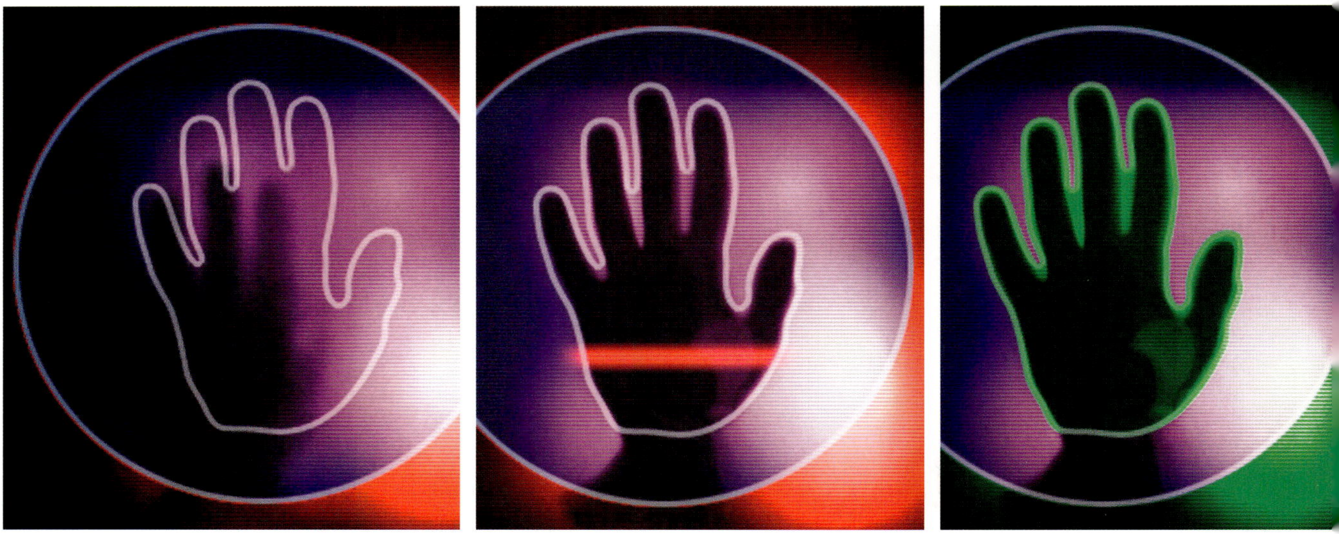

The psi garden is a technology-lover's haven – the ultimate 'intelligent' environment. It's for people who want to be the first to own the latest innovations, who understand the potential of technology and enjoy maximising its use. Technology is time-saving, of course, so it can be a good solution for the garden lover who wants, or needs, to be able to sit back and let the garden look after itself rather than get too involved with all that heavy manual work. But even the most technological garden will still have to deal with nature to a certain degree and can never be completely maintenance-free. This garden is about more than simply saving time and labour, though; it's also about taking real pleasure in being surrounded by smart, cool, green-living gadgetry. In fact, in the most effective psi gardens, technology will work hand-in-hand with its surroundings. The psi garden represents man, nature and machine working together in harmony.

Linking the home and garden

The garden can be connected up to the house, so that the transition from indoors to outdoors is seamless and the overall living environment functions in the most efficient way. It is easy to live as comfortably and as conveniently outdoors as it is indoors. For example, you could install data points (where laptop or hand-held computers can be plugged in) outside to catch up with work, an outdoor entertainment system, and a bar for relaxation and play. Current technology makes advanced lighting systems linked to the home and garden a real possibility. You can connect up the whole system to a computer that will remember light settings and atmospheres for different

'Although garden technology has not quite caught up with technology for the home, I'm sure it won't be long until it does.'

moods. In theory, it could also be linked to a solar panel on the roof of an out building that would power, or assist in powering, all the workings of the garden (see overleaf for more about lighting).

The garden's style is sleek, controlled, and futuristic; the hard landscaping is bold and there are many dramatic features to reflect its state-of-the-art design.

All the comforts of home

I suppose anything is possible within the psi garden, depending on how much money you are willing to spend. There are companies who will tailor the garden for you according to your specifications. Think about what is achievable for inside space with state-of-the-art technology, remote control atmospheric lighting, hidden music systems, plasma screen TVs, walls that can be moved to alter the dimensions of the space. Theoretically, all these

I have often thought about what I would put in a technologically sophisticated psi garden. If you let your imagination run wild, there are certainly plenty of possibilities. One idea I would love to try out is to have a deck or seating area that would automatically follow the sun around the garden on a system of tracks. It could be remotely operated, too. You could even lay a lawn in a self-contained pan that would be moved around the garden on tracks.

things are possible for outside space too. Although garden technology has not quite caught up with technology for the home, I'm sure it won't be long until it does, since the garden's role is changing so that it is more important to everyday life. With space at such a premium, people now want to utilize all available space to the maximum. So the garden now needs to have all the comforts and convenience of the home.

It could be possible to have a canopy or awning that would automatically cover a seating area when it senses rain. One of my favourite ideas is to have lighting that would 'fade up' when someone was there and then 'fade down' when they left. This would create the fantastic effect of lighting you up when you walked around the space. With heat sensors or pressure sensors underfoot, this would be relatively easy to do. I love the idea of a garden in which all the areas could be moved to change the overall look for different occasions; even rooms at the back of the house could have retractable roofs to extend the inside of the house out into the garden. It's the same idea you find in those picture games with the sliding tiles, but on a larger scale. It's a wild concept but it is possible. You could even have moving screens that alter the space and create different areas that are truly adaptable for any circumstance. I know these are fantastical ideas and probably way

beyond the budget available to most of us, but this garden is about pushing the boundaries to create an interactive space that suits your needs.

Irrigation systems

Irrigation systems are the ultimate in time-saving devices for the garden. They can be designed specifically for each garden and the individual needs of the lawn as well as almost every plant in it. Flower beds are watered automatically and only when necessary. You can also programme a computer to control how often and how much water the garden gets. It is within the realm of possibility that, using moisture sensors in the soil, the system could even adjust to the environment and the seasons to prevent over- or under-watering.

'A really clever innovation is the robotic lawn mower that cuts the lawn for you. It's battery-powered and suitable for most small-to medium-sized gardens. You run a wire around the edges of the lawn, including around island beds with trees, and then quite simply let the mower get on with the job.'

The robotic lawn mower

A really clever innovation is the robotic lawn mower that cuts the lawn for you. It's battery-powered and suitable for most small-to medium-sized gardens. You run a wire around the edges of the lawn, including around island beds with trees, and then quite simply let the mower get on with the job. There's a re-charging station where the mower can dock to recharge (which takes a whole day), and then continue its cutting again. Although it takes longer than you would to cut the lawn manually, it's perfect for those who like to spend the weekend enjoying the garden rather than maintaining it.

Music

The garden is a great place to enjoy music but harsh weather conditions and the cold aren't really ideal for ordinary speakers. So someone developed a range of speakers that can take all the outdoors can throw at them. There's nothing better than sitting in the hot tub chilling with Kylie, enjoying a barbecue with the Sex Pistols, or relaxing on the lawn with Mozart, and now all this is possible – no need to move your speakers to the nearest window just to hear some music in the garden.

Choosing a design

The design of the garden itself should aim to accommodate these technologies. The type of person this garden will typically appeal to will have modern tastes and the style of their home will be contemporary. The garden should be a reflection of this with clean, pale colours such as blues, greys (stone), creams, and whites. Any bright colour will stand out like a sore thumb and detract from the clean look. I think the garden should still have traditional features such as hidden seating areas and perhaps even a pergola walkway,

but the space should generally be regarded as somewhere for innovation and challenging norms.

Materials and focal points

Hard materials that would suit seating areas and paths include granite, slate, smooth sandstone pavers, tiles, and even smaller units like block pavers and setts. Try to use big, bold shapes to define areas in the garden. This will give each of these areas a sense of purpose, and by surrounding them with walls of planting you will create a real sense of seclusion. Such areas will surely be spaces that you'll want to show off, so create some eye-catching focal points that perhaps verge on the unusual: sculptures, water features, or even architectural plants in unusual containers, will work well.

'A psi garden is not just for adults; children love anything visually and mentally stimulating. You could create an area of the garden to be a sensory playground (which both adults and children will love). This might include a statue that spurts water at you when you walk past, strange lighting effects and smoke machines for water features.'

Children

A psi garden is not just for adults; children love anything visually and mentally stimulating. You could create an area of the garden to be a sensory playground (which both adults and children will love). This might include a statue that spurts water at you when you walk past, strange lighting effects, and smoke machines for water features. You could even create an outdoor disco

for kids (or adults!) with music, disco balls, and coloured lighting. Knowing what kids are like, they will probably find the robotic lawn mower fascinating, too!

Designing a small building

An outdoor studio or room would work well in this garden, either as an office or as a recreation room. I've often fantasised about having a space in the garden for an escape, where there was a pool table, table tennis, arcade games, a bar, or even a cinema projector (I'm dreaming again! More realistically, it would have to be a space to enable me to work at my designs). Just think of the possibilities. I am not talking about a shed with an old telly in the corner, but a carefully designed, small building that works with the landscape you are creating. So consider materials such as glass, wood, or steel in your plan. Plant around the building carefully so it sits comfortably within the space. If you work from home, imagine how terrific it would be to get away from the house and sit in a fully-kitted-out office set amongst the beauty of your garden. A building that is almost transparent works well in this kind of space; glass has qualities that will allow the structure to blend into its surroundings. This is important because if it is too solid-looking it will dominate the garden and draw too much attention to itself. You need permission from your local planning office to build any permanent structures in the garden, so you will have to get application forms and provide them with the full plans for your proposal.

You may also want to read the sections in this book called the easy garden, the socialising garden, and the designer garden for more suggestions and ideas.

Planting list

Acers
Bamboos
Carex
Choisya ternata
Cordylines
Cotinus coggygria 'Royal Purple'
Dicksonia fibrosa
Ferns
Mahonia japonica
Miscanthus
Nandina domestica
Pennisetum
Phoenix canariensis
Phormiums
Trachycarpus fortunei
Viburnum tinus
Yucca

Miscanthus

Viburnum tinus

the know-how

Patios

Before you start
First of all, using string and pegs, mark the area where you want the patio to be and have the string at the same level you want the finished patio to be at. It's essential to slope the patio away from the house to ensure that rain water doesn't collect by the walls. Otherwise you will end up with damp problems. Set the string line so it falls about 25 mm every 1.5 m as you move away from the house and this will give you a fall of about 1:60. Also ensure that the patio is two bricks or 150 mm below the damp proof course (DPC) of the house. Damp proof courses usually can be seen as a black membrane in the joint between the bricks, a black tar-like layer, or sometimes on older houses it will be slate.

Preparing the area
Using the string, which is the finished paving level, dig out the depth needed for the overall patio construction. Allow 100–150mm for the hardcore sub-base which can be made up of broken old bricks and lumps of concrete. Then allow for 50 mm of sharp sand and the depth of the paving, usually 35–50 mm. The thickness of the sub-base will depend on the ground conditions; the softer the ground, the deeper the sub-base needs to be. The sub-base and sharp sand will, in turn, need compacting. Normally, these materials compact to approximately 2/3 of their original depth.

Preparing the paving
The mix on which to lay the paving is usually between 3:1 and 5:1 sand : cement. Add enough water so that the mix has a nice 'workable' consistency. To lay the slab, put five blobs of mortar, one on each corner and one in the middle of each slab. The blobs should be big enough that when you tamp the slab down they come together; with larger slabs you may need more blobs of mix.

Laying the paving
There are many different patterns for laying paving so plan exactly what you want the end effect to be. Place each flag carefully, adjusting the position to your outline and anticipated pattern. Tap down until level with the proposed final level using a rubber mallet. Allow for the direction of the fall away from the house. This is far easier if you use a spirit level. Allow approximately a 10 mm space or joint width between two adjacent flags. When you have finished, it is important to tidy around any exposed edges at the front and on the sides of the patio. To create a neat finish after laying the patio, 'haunch' the edges at an angle of about 45° from just under the slab to ground level.

Finishing
Wait for the bedding mortar to dry (usually 24 hours) before beginning to fill the joints. Use the same proportions of sand and cement when laying the patio but I suggest keeping the mix a bit dryer than before so you don't stain the slabs. Fill all the joints using a small pointing trowel, and then smooth over using the trowel. You can buy special pointing irons for the job or even a bit of cut-off hose will work. Be sure to push as much mix as you can into the gaps to create a solid, impervious joint. Then once it's dry, you're done!

There are, of course, alternatives to laying a straight old patio; you could stagger the edges by leaving slabs out and adding extras to the sides or a more irregular shape. You can leave slabs out for planting: turf, herbs, and grasses work well. Or you could even leave slightly bigger pointing gaps and use fine gravel instead of mortar for a different effect.

Decks

A deck is quite a simple thing to build, and you can do it yourself if you want to. It consists of a timber frame, usually made from 4 inch by 2 inch treated timber, and decking boards, which are screwed onto the frame.

Making a square deck

For a simple square deck, you will need to make the outer square of the frame secure with screws in the corners, and then insert the joists spaced no further apart than 80 cm. If they are any wider than this, you'll end up with a bouncy deck. Next insert small noggins to act as extra support to the frame. This will produce a large grid onto which the decking can be attached.

Supports for decks

Decks can be built sitting on a solid surface such as concrete, erected on posts, or placed on blocks. Wood in contact with soil will rot quickly. Any kind of support should be evenly spaced, to hold the deck in place, and close enough together so that the whole structure is sturdy with no springiness. Posts should be sunk into holes at least a foot deep and bedded with concrete. This guide is only intended for decks built on the ground. For any for more complex jobs, such as raised decks, seek professional guidance.

Preparation for laying the deck

You should put a layer of landscape fabric, and then a layer of gravel, under the deck to stop the weeds growing up between the decking boards. Also ensure that any cuts you need to make on the timber are treated with a wood preservative to prevent rotting.

It's always best to screw the decking boards to the frame because wood tends to warp, which can pull nails out. Also ensure all fixings are suitable for outdoor use and that they won't rust. When attaching the boards, counter-sink the holes before drilling and screwing so that the screw heads are not sticking out. This is important as it will prevent anyone from cutting their feet when walking on them. You also need to treat the screw holes with preservative to help prevent rot.

Laying the decking boards

The decking boards need to be laid with about a 5–8 mm gap between them to allow for the wood to expand and contract. When finished, treat the wood with a stain or wood preservative, which will extend the life span, and repeat the treatment every year.

Ponds and water features

You'll find water features in all different shapes and sizes, and most will come with instructions on how to build them. But you can also make your own and be original.

What you need

All you need is a pump and a sump and you can come up with all sorts of cool ideas. At shows, we have made water features out of aluminium air conditioning tubes, flower pots, and all sorts of weird things! You can also have fountains, streams, waterfalls and an assortment of complex features. However, I would suggest getting a specialist in for these because a badly made water feature can ruin a space.

If you are going to make a pond, you will need a hole, or if it is a raised pond, then some kind of wall to retain it. I made one out of sleepers once that looked fantastic. You can buy rigid pond liners at garden centres but they are already formed so there is no scope for change; the best option is to get a good, strong, flexible pond liner.

Using the pond liner
Once you have dug your hole, you should line the bottom and sides with a 5-7 cm layer of sand; this will stop stones and roots puncturing the liner. Next, stretch the liner over the hole and support it all around with heavy bricks or pavers, then put the hose in the middle and turn on the water. The liner will fill up slowly and the weight will sink the liner into the hole, moulding to the shape of it perfectly. When it is full, turn the hose off. Then cut the excess liner away, leaving a good 30 cm or so extra around the edges.

The final look of the pond
You will need to find a way to hide the excess liner; the final look of the pond depends very much on how it is finished. You can grade the pond edges, gently sloping them downward, and then cover the liner with pebbles and gravel to give it a natural effect, which would also provide access to the pond for wildlife. You can pave around the edges, to create more of a formal pool. Or you could build a deck around it to create a serene, still pool in the middle of a jungle oasis. It is up to you and will depend very much on the overall design of your garden.

Be careful where you position any pool keep it away from trees because there is nothing worse than leaves falling into the pond to make it a stagnant, stinking mess. There are too many possibilities to list in this small section of the book, so I would suggest further reading on the subject of ponds.

Pergolas and arches

You can buy ready-made pergolas and arches in garden centres, but they are also easy to make. You can buy arches constructed from metal tubing that is bent to shape; these are really easy to put together and make great features in any garden. Pergolas are ideal for spanning walkways or for creating shaded seating areas. Pergolas are simple timber frameworks, notched and screwed together, and supported by upright timbers that are set in concrete. For a rustic effect, use round poles half notched together and supported on round uprights in the same way. A lean-to pergola is supported on one side by a building. This can be a great way of creating shade near the house and creating a visual link between house and garden. A lean-to is basically half a pergola that is supported by either joist hangers or timber attached to the wall.

Steps

You can use a variety of materials to create steps in your garden, of brick, timber or natural stone, and your choice of material will be influenced by the style of garden you are creating. The simplest method is to use a length of log as the riser and then secure it in position with pegs and backfill, with either gravel or bark chip. Steps like these work better in an informal setting. Brick steps create a neater effect; the work involved to make them is far greater but they will last longer than a timber construction. The risers are constructed much like a low brick wall and the treads can be either brick, concrete or natural stone slabs. It's important that the tread slopes away from the risers slightly so water can run off. Steps do not always have to go straight up or down; it is effective if there is a change in direction or, if there are a lot of steps, it is often nice to include a landing as a place to rest, where you could even include a bench.

Walls

Bricks
As with steps, there are a variety of materials suitable for building walls. Brick is the most common, as it is widely available and relatively cheap. It is important to choose bricks similar to those in your house to create a visual link. There are a number of different bonds you can use to build your wall: English bond and Flemish bond are common. It's best if the brick walls in a garden are constructed two bricks wide, a method called a double-skinned wall. Laying bricks is actually quite an easy process but it does take a bit of time and practice. Bricks are laid on a mortar mix of six parts soft sand to one part cement, all on top of a concrete foundation. A damp-proof membrane should be installed about 15 cm above ground level to stop rising damp. Lay the first and last brick on the first courses and run a string line between them to ensure a straight, level wall; use a level as you continue laying the bricks. Laying a course of bricks on edge like soldiers laying down in a row finishes the wall off nicely. When you are done, you will need to clean the front of the wall of any excess mortar and then point the joints neatly with a pointing trowel or a cut-off section of hose.

Concrete blocks
Concrete blocks are a very useful walling material because they are large, strong and quick to lay. They are also really quite cheap and easier to build with than brick. They are usually finished with a layer of render and then painted, but you could texture the finish with a brush or sponge. They are laid in the same way as a brick wall, but they take less than half the time to erect. A slightly stiffer mix of mortar may help, due to the extra weight of the blocks.

Timber
Timber is often used for walls, too. The best options are heavy timbers such as new railway sleepers and telegraph poles. They are also already treated, which will make them last for years and require little care. Because they are so heavy, they can be laid onto compacted ground and built up alternately like the bricks in a wall. You can buy fixings called 'timber fixings' that will hold them together without the need for drilling. For extra support, iron rods or timber posts set in concrete can be installed on the hidden side.

Other materials
There are numerous other solid walling components that you can use, ranging from natural stone to concrete products which have been made to look like real stone, or specially created blocks that stack together needing no mortar at all. Look around and consider all the options.

Lawns

Undoubtedly, a well kept-lawn is a real asset to any garden and, raised from seed, they are much cheaper than laying turf. But most of us are too impatient to wait so laying a lawn is often the only answer. When buying turf, get it from a good reputable source, because the quality of the turf will be reflected in the finished lawn. Usually turf comes in rolls that cover 1 square metre, but if you are covering a large area it is worth spending a bit more on massive rolls that can be laid using a special tractor. Preparation is the key. The ground should be as level as possible with all the stones and roots removed, and you should ensure there are no lumps or bumps. Anything left like that will just show through when you lay the lawn. As you lay it, stagger the joints and knead the turfs together around the edges; always walk along boards so as not to tread on the freshly laid turf or your carefully prepared ground. Once the job is finished it will need plenty of water, otherwise the turfs will shrink. Make sure you (and any children or animals!) keep off the lawn until it has well rooted. This could take anywhere from two weeks to a month or more. Also keep watering the new lawn, especially during summer. It is best to do this at dusk, otherwise the hot sun will evaporate the water. You could consider leaving the sprinkler on all night.

Lighting in the garden

You can get simple-to-install kits in garden centres, which are fine for a quick fix solution. But for a more impressive lighting system you will need to get a professional to install it. There are two types of lighting for the garden: functional and accent.

Functional and accent lighting

Functional lighting is used in outbuildings, or for social spaces, such as eating and play areas. It would also be used for safety reasons, to illuminate steps or paths. Use spread lights for walkways, for they provide a pool of light with a wide beam. Functional lighting is also used for security purposes; lights triggered by sensors will act as a deterrent to intruders.

Accent lighting is used to make a feature of a certain plant or a focal point in the garden. Accent light could be fairy lights in a tree or a floodlight placed at ground level to silhouette a tree. It's best to keep accent lighting to a minimum to get maximum effect. Too many accent lights will detract from each other. It is also best to stick to white light, or one coloured light which will enhance the natural colours of a plant. Coloured lights create an unnatural atmosphere, more like a stage set than a garden.

There are different ways in which to use accent lighting:

1. Up-lighting: light placed to face upward, from the base of a plant or object.
2. Moonlighting: a light or system of lights is suspended in a tree, pointing down, to spread soft light like the moon.
3. Spotlighting: a spot light is used to draw attention to a feature in the garden.
4. Silhouetting: back-lighting to create a silhouette of a plant or feature.
5. Shadowing: positioning a light to create interesting shadows on a wall.

LED lights

Garden lighting is becoming more and more advanced these days. Fibre optics can now be used in the garden o create an effect like a system of stars howing up through a deck, and LED ighting is now available for use as ecess lights in a deck or patio. LED ights are great because they create a lear bright light, and each one will last or about 100,000 hours before needing o be changed.

ositioning the lights

inally, when positioning lights it is mportant to position them to avoid lare. Make sure that all the lights are ointing away from areas such as atios, paths and decks in such a way hat they are lighting features and not our eyes.

Finding a reputable contractor

Many people will lack the confidence to tackle DIY jobs in the garden for themselves. The alternative is to find some trustworthy qualified professionals but this can be a bit of a mission and there are pitfalls. So here are some tips to consider when you are thinking of transforming your garden and looking for some help to do it.

Plan early

The demand for landscaped gardens is now so high that many 'good' landscape contractors will be booked up for weeks or even months. So plan the garden 2 or 3 months in advance of when you want the work to begin, and allow a few weeks for the contractor to source materials and prepare for the job.

Seek several quotations

Never accept an 'estimate'. Get at least three quotations to establish the correct rate for the project. Don't necessarily rule out the cheapest option but do ensure that installation is to the same specification as the more expensive installers.

Find a contractor

The best way to find a contractor is by word of mouth from friends or family but unless you or your friends have had first-hand experience of a reliable installer, consider appointing a Marshalls Register contractor. All Marshalls Register contractors are regularly assessed and have a signed code of practice, agreeing to carry out installations in accordance with Marshalls' installation specification. Of course price will, ultimately, swing your decision but it is also important to choose the contractor you feel most comfortable with and one who understands what you are aiming for with the finished garden. A good contractor will listen to your ideas and work closely with you offering their expertise to create an end product you are happy with – they will know what products are most suitable and will guide you through design and construction to achieve the best result. For details of Marshalls' Register contractors in your area, log onto *www.marshalls.co.uk/drivesandgardens* or call the Marshalls' Helpline: 0870 120 7474. A word of warning: try to avoid contractors who only advertise with a mobile number – a home or office number provides a fixed address which makes it more difficult to rip you off, which unfortunately some dodgy companies do.

Insist on a formal contract

Once the work and quote have been agreed, insist on a formal contract to prevent misunderstandings further down the line. All works to be undertaken should be listed in the contract, and there will usually be a clause to cover the contractor for unexpected circumstances (if they find a bomb shelter buried where the pond, was going to be it will cost more to remove it) so have a little extra cash stashed away somewhere just in case.

Request a guarantee

All Register members are able to provide homeowners with a unique, ısurance-backed, 10-year guarantee pon request, covering both the roduct and the workmanship for the ıll period. The guarantee is assignable ɔ the new owner if you sell your home, 's valid if the contractor ceases trading r if the contractor is still in business ut is unable to honour his obligation. lot all contractors will offer such uarantees, but try to get something vritten into the contract to cover any uilding work in the garden if anything hould go wrong. It will be difficult to et any contractor to guarantee the lants because there are so many arying factors associated with plant urvival, so make sure that the plants ısed are good quality and healthy-ooking in the first place.

Timber merchants

nternational timber – For great wood!
Haven road
The Hythe
Colchester
Essex
C02 8HU
01206 866 822

My design company

Pro Create uk ltd
01206 767726
E mail: Info@procreate.co.uk

Plants

Hearts Delight
Long Road
Lawford
Manningtee
Essex
CO11 2EF

The place for plants! (That is the name)

East Bergholt place
East Bergholt
Suffolk
C07 6UP
Tel: 01206 299 224

For organic worm compost

Willis Worms
The Mount
Bull Lane
Bishops Castle
SY9 5DA
www.willisworms.co.uk
Tel: 07788690553

For bespoke glass work

Alm glassworks
unit 4E
Riverside Avenue West
Lawford
Manningtree
Esex
C011 1UX
Tel: 1206 398003

Paints and stains

Johnstones Decorating centre
Unit 4
Mason road
Cowdray Centre
Colchester
Essex
CO1 1BX
Tel: 01206 560928

index

Compiled by INDEXING SPECIALISTS (UK) Ltd

acknowledgements

I would like to thank Marshalls plc, the UK's leading manufacturer of concrete, clay and natural stone paving products for letting me have the opportunity to interpret their nine months of research, which was conducted in association with the specialist forecasters at Dragon, an independent international brand agency. This research looked at future lifestyle trends and how these trends will affect what homeowners want from their gardens and how they want to use them.

I was able to translate the insights into tomorrow's society into ideas, practical advice, and techniques for creating any one of the ten garden themes that homeowners will be able to integrate seamlessly into their lifestyles, creating gardens that they can live in today and enjoy well into the future.

Marshalls' innovative paving products help homeowners transform an outdoor area into their dream garden. Call 0870 120 7474 for a brochure or visit their website *www.marshalls.co.uk/transform* for inspiration, ideas, and information about professional contractors and local merchants and stockists.

If you would like any information on finding a professional installer, or on the paving that is featured within the book and where you can buy it from, call 0870 120 7474 or visit *www.marshalls.co.uk.* Click on 'Home & Garden', and then enter 'Customer Service'. From here you can enter your post code into 'Find Approved Contractors' or 'Stockist Search' to find the nearest professional installers in your area and your local stockist or merchant. It is quick, simple, and reliable.

I would also like to thank Xternal dimensions who have supplied images for the book. Xternal dimensions design and build gardens and driveways. They employ their own in-house landscape designers and construction teams and were RHS award winners in 2001, 2002, and 2003. For further information call: 0870 240 7067, email: service@xdl.co.uk or *www.xdl.co.uk* or visit their inspirational display centres at Lichfield Stratford, and Knutsford in Cheshire.

And finally, I would like to thank Nick Thorogood, Chantal Rutherford Browne Dorita Hollins, and Tamsyn Zietsman at UK Style; Richard Farmbrough and all the 'Model Gardens' team at Reef Television; Janice Gabriel at Endemol UK; Alison Sharman and Dominic Vallely at the BBC; Jez Felwick and Rhian Evans, my long suffering agents at Form (Talent) Ltd; Jamie Goodman for making me look good; and all my family.